Battles in the Clouds

Battles in the Clouds
Accounts of Conflicts in the Sky during the First World War

ILLUSTRATED

J Humphrey Lewis

LEONAUR

Battles in the Clouds
Accounts of Conflicts in the Sky during the First World War
by J Humphrey Lewis

FIRST EDITION

ILLUSTRATED

Leonaur is an imprint of Oakpast Ltd
Copyright in this form © 2017 Oakpast Ltd

ISBN: 978-1-78282-658-3 (hardcover)
ISBN: 978-1-78282-659-0 (softcover)

http://www.leonaur.com

Publisher's Notes

The views expressed in this book are not necessarily those of the publisher.

Contents

A Battle in the Air	7
Turning Heavens into Hell—Exploits of Canadian Flying Corps	11
The Skill of British Airmen	17
Airmen in the Deserts of Egypt	25
Deeds of Heroism and Daring	31
An Aviator's Story of Bombarding the Enemy	149
A Bombing Expedition with the British Air Service	153
Lost on a Seaplane and Set Adrift in a Mine-Field	161
The Ghastly Havoc Wrought by the Air-Demons	169
"Flying for France"—Hero Tales of Battles in the Air	175
Knights of the Air—Frenchmen Who Defy Death	203
Tales of German Air Raiders over London and Paris	211
The Aerial Attack on Ravenna	219

A Battle in the Air
By Logan Marshall

How Zeppelin and Aeroplane Fight for Supremacy

Out of the grey dawn mist the huge pencilled Zeppelin emerges, her engines thrashing fiercely. She is late in getting back from her night raid, and the captain has seen two ominous black spots in the sky to the rearward.

Aeroplanes! Since the news of the night raid was flashed to the Allies aerial stations men and machines have been preparing for the grim task of intercepting the Zeppelin on the return journey, when daylight would give aeroplanes their full power of attack. While it is yet dark two of the most daring pilots start, and by clever airmanship they make a course which should give them a strategic position when the Zeppelin appears.

But the crafty enemy has taken another course, and when dawn breaks he is not to be seen by the aerial watchers. Masses of fleecy clouds render observation difficult, and hope has almost disappeared when suddenly one of the pilots sees the Zeppelin loom through a cloud bank several miles ahead. Heeling over at a terrific angle, the little craft swing round in pursuit, climbing as they go so as to get the "hawk position" over the enemy ship.

Hunting Their Prey

The Zeppelin has disappeared! Somewhere in that upper world of coldness and rudely-disturbed silence the ship is traveling through billowy clouds, now touched by the glorious lights of the new day. A reek of burned oil fouls the pure air, and the roar of engines in full throttle pulsates into space.

Like swallows in pursuit of flies the aeroplanes hunt high and low for the enemy, and not until after one long despairing dive to earth is the vessel sighted. It has cleverly been using the clouds for cover, and by the liberal sacrifice of gas and ballast it has danced up and down in the air to elude the hunters. In these tactics, the Zeppelin has the advantage of quick movements. A brilliant burst of sunlight suddenly reveals the ship to the aviators, and the Zeppelin captain also discovers the enemy as they wheel round to pursue. The aeroplanes are at a lower level, and they promptly start climbing. The Zeppelin leaps upwards, and setting her elevation planes seeks to gain a still greater advantage in height.

How They Avoid the Zeppelin's Fire

It looks as if pursuit were hopeless, but the aeroplanes hold on grimly. Steadily they gain in forward speed. Their engines are fresh, whilst the Zeppelin motors are feeling the long strain of high-speed running. When the affair settles into a stern chase the Zeppelin guns open fire. The airmen are prepared for this and keep as close as possible in the wake of the German ship, thus masking the guns in the forward cabin. But the Zeppelin, learning a lesson from previous encounters, has guns in the rear cabin, and despite the disadvantage of shooting in a line parallel with the keel they make rapid practice on the aeroplanes. Now the situation is growing desperate for the Zeppelin. All the ballast has been thrown out, petrol is running short, and the engines are showing signs of increasing weakness and irregular running. The engineers mutter and make signs to each other.

Undeterred by the guns, one aeroplane has already climbed to the same level as the airship and is steadily rising to a height where it will be concealed from the Zeppelin guns by the body of the ship itself. This Zeppelin has tried and discarded the gun-mounting on the top of the ship, and the captain can only storm with impotent rage as the aeroplane climbs to a higher level. A great burst of forward speed can alone save him from being overtaken by the enemy.

Now the second aeroplane has risen also above the fire zone, though one ragged wing shows a wound. As a balloon, the Zeppelin can rise no higher, for all her ballast has been sacrificed, and the captain decides to bring his elevating planes back to the normal and stake all on a high-speed flight in a horizontal course. He is encouraged in this by the sight of the German lines below him with the landmarks which he knows so well. Puffs of smoke tell him that the aeroplanes are being shelled by German gunners, who very quickly have guessed what the situation is. Some of the shells burst so close to him that his opinion of the gunners is not flattering, and yet he knows that if something is not done to the airmen he is doomed.

READY FOR THE FINAL BLOW

The firing soon ceases. A few moments of intense agony follow as the crew look at each other with horror-stricken eyes. What is happening above them?

From their little cabins, there is no possibility of an upward survey, for the great body of the ship looms above them, shutting out the overhead view. But they can picture those two gaunt birds flying after them remorselessly as Fate, and inch by inch gaining upon them. When the Zeppelin lies beneath the aeroplanes a bomb will drop on the ship's back, and then—

In a frenzy, the captain plunges the ship downward and swings her to the right with a swerve which threatens to break her spine. But the elephantine manoeuvre avails little. The birds above him can dive and swerve with the grace of swallows whilst his giant ship lumbers like a derelict balloon.

"Harbour!" shouts one of the crew, pointing to the familiar long building far below. In the coolness of despair the man levels his glasses, and he discerns men running and signalling.

A wireless message is picked up by the Zeppelin operator—"Two aeroplanes above you."

The captain suddenly falls into a seat, burying his face in his hands and sobbing hysterically. His nerve has broken.

"How long they are!" yells a stolid fellow looking upward.

But as he speaks there is a dull thud, and then a sheet of flame, spreading with lightning speed, envelops them. The burning hydrogen consumes them with appalling fury, and in a few instants the great ship, crumbling and melting, hurtles to earth like a blazing meteor.

From the earth, many guns speak. They but serve for the firing salute over the graves of the fallen.

Two black specks in the sky rock under the concussions of the bursting shells, but keep on their way.

A few instants later the sickening crash of the Zeppelin carcass paralyzes the gunners with horror. Only a German knows what it is to see a Zeppelin fall. It is an omen of doom.

Turning Heavens into Hell—Exploits of Canadian Flying Corps

BATTLE IN AIR WITH ONE HUNDRED AEROPLANES
Told by Officer of Royal Canadian Flying Corps

The heroism of the Canadians is one of the immortal epics of the War. The great dominion sent across the seas her strongest sons. Their valour in trench and field "saved the British army" on many critical moments. The feats of daring of these Canadians would fill many volumes, but here is one story typical of their sublime courage—a tale of the air.

1—WITH THE CANADIANS IN THE CLOUDS

There were one hundred of us—fifty on a side—but we turned the heavens into a hell, up in the air there, more terrible than ten thousand devils could have made running rampant in the pit.

The sky blazed and crackled with bursting time bombs, and the machine guns spitted out their steel venom, while underneath us hung what seemed like a net of fire, where shells from the Archies, vainly trying to reach us, were bursting.

We had gone out early in the morning, fifty of us, from the Royal Canadian Flying Corps barracks, back of the lines, when the sun was low and my courage lower, to bomb the Prussian trenches before the infantry should attack.

Our machines were stretched out across a flat tableland. Here and there in little groups the pilots were receiving instructions from their commander and consulting maps and photographs.

At last we all climbed into our machines. All along the line engines began to roar and sputter. Here was a 300 horsepower Rolls-Royce, with a mighty, throbbing voice; over there a $10,000 Larone rotary engine vieing with the others in making a noise. Then there were the little fellows humming and spitting the "vipers" or "maggots," as they are known in the service.

At last the squadron commander took his place in his machine and rose with a whirr. The rest of us rose and circled round, getting our formation.

Crack! At the signal from the commander's pistol we darted forward, going ever higher and higher, while the cheers of the mechanicians and riggers grew fainter.

Across our own trenches we sailed and out over No Man's Land, like a huge, eyeless, pock-scarred earth face staring up at us.

There was another signal from the commander. Down we swooped. The bomb racks rattled as hundreds of bombs were let loose, and a second later came the crackle of their explosions over the heads of the Boches in their trenches.

Lower and lower we flew. We skimmed the trenches and sprayed bullets from our machine guns. The crashing of the weapons drowned the roar of the engines.

I saw ahead of me a column of flame shoot up from one of our machines, and I caught a momentary glance at the pilot's face. It was greenish-ash colour. His petrol tank had been hit. I hope the fall killed him and that he did not burn to death.

2—The Vultures Over the Trenches

Away in the distance a number of specks had risen, like vultures scenting the carrion that had already been made. It was a German squadron. The Archies had not bothered us much while we were spraying the Prussian trenches, but now we had that other squadron to take care of. Our orders were to bomb the trenches. We could not spare a bomb or a cartridge from the task of putting the fear of Britain into the hearts of the infantry below before our own "Tommies" should start over the top.

I don't know what it was, but suddenly, just after my partner had let go a rack of bombs, there was a terrific explosion just beneath us. My machine leaped upward, twisted, then dropped suddenly. Death himself was trying to wrench the control levers from my grip, but I clung to them madly and we righted. A few inches more and I couldn't have told you about this.

There was no longer any chance to worry about flying position. There were too many things occupying my attention—that line of grey down there that we were trying to erase and the Boche squadron thrumming down on us.

One drum of our ammunition was already used up. My partner whirled around on his stool—a sort of piano stool, which always made me think of the tuneless, tinpanny instrument back in quarters—grabbed another drum and slammed it into the machine gun. It was to be a parting message for the Prussians, for the commander was just signalling to retire.

My partner lurched forward. He was hit. A thin red stream trickled down his face.

I raced westward, the air whistling through the bullet holes in the wings of the machine and my partner leaning against the empty bomb rack, silent.

As we sailed over the foremost Prussian trench some Scotch were just leaping into it. The "ladies from hell" the Germans call them, because of their kilts.

Several machines had landed before I took the ground. Ambulances were dashing back and forth across the flying field.

They lifted my partner out of the aeroplane, but they did not put him into an ambulance. He had answered another recall. I walked to quarters ill—ill at heart, at stomach, at mind. I'll never know a better pal than was Tom.

On the way, I managed to help with a machine that had just landed. A big Rolls-Royce it was, and the radiator had been hit by a bit of shrapnel. The pilot and observer were both terribly scalded.

Just by the aerodrome another biplane fluttered down. The observer was dead. The pilot was hit in a dozen places. Somehow, he brought the machine in, switched off his engine and slopped forward in his seat, stone dead.

Ten minutes later I was sound asleep. The next day we were at it again.

In battles of this kind it is more or less a matter of good fortune if you escape with your life. Flying ability and trickiness can play but little part. It is in the lone adventure that stunt flying helps.

3—The Mysterious Major and the Uhlans

One of the most versatile flyers in the corps was the "Mysterious Major." Condon was his name, but to all the men, both sides of No Man's Land, he was the "Mysterious Major."

He was forced to glide to earth one day, back of the Prussian lines, with his big motor stalled. He leaped out hastily, adjusted a bit of machinery and spun the propellers. A gentle purr, then silence, was the response.

Once more he flashed the blades around, with no better result.

It wasn't a healthy neighbourhood to be in. With a short, crisp oath, the "Mysterious Major" set to work in dead earnest. Down the road to the right of the field a cloud of dust, flying high, appeared. It meant cavalry. The major's ears caught the sound of hoofbeats.

It was tradition that he would never be killed in the air, but here he was on earth, with cavalry galloping toward him. His descent had probably been spotted and the Uhlans sent to get him.

At last he got a roar from the engine that sounded like business, but it petered out.

Closer came the hoof beats. The Uhlans rode over a fence and came galloping across the field. A shot punctuated his exhortations to the motor and slit one of the planes.

Pulling and tugging, he got his machine turned so that he could use his machine gun. *Br-r-rang!* He let drive a drum of ammunition from his machine gun. He saw several horses and riders go down in sprawling, rolling heaps, then turned to his motor again.

Eight or ten Uhlans who had escaped his murderous fire withdrew. He knew what they would do. They would return from every side at once, and his single machine gun could never stop them.

If he could only get into the air he would feel safe. Once more he twisted the propeller. As though nothing had ever been wrong, the engine started to thrum and roar. He leaped into the seat.

Quickly the machine rose. The Uhlans saw it. I suppose they knew he had not loaded the machine gun again, and they galloped on to the field, firing at him.

He was so low that there was every chance for them to hit his petrol tank or even the major himself. So, he went even lower. Straight at the heads of the horses he drove. The animals, scared at the great, white-winged, roaring machine, reared and plunged, throwing some of the riders to the ground. The others were too busy with their mounts to shoot straight.

The major waved goodbye, fired a couple of parting shots from his service revolver and climbed to where the bullets could not reach him. It was not his fate to die in the air, he thought, but only a few weeks after he told me this story he was killed by a shrapnel burst from an Archie, which wrecked his machine while he was flying with an air patrol.

I do not think they ever should have sent him on such work. He was too valuable alone. The Prussians feared him so much that a price was upon his head.

Scarcely a day went by that some new feat of daring was not accredited to this almost phantom-like flier. Perhaps he did not perform them all, but the effect was cumulative.

I have known the "Mysterious Major" to side slip three thousand feet at a time. He used to skim so close to the Boche trenches that they say men ducked their heads, and all the time he was pouring six hundred shots a minute from his machine gun.

Many said the "Mysterious Major" was crazy, but if we all were suffering from the same dementia the Boches wouldn't be able to show their heads. He was of inestimable value to the secret service, but those stories will have to wait until after the war, if they are ever told.

4—The Birdman Who Played 'Possum

One of the most thrilling encounters I can recall is that of Captain Woodhouse, who, accompanied by another pilot, was out over the Prussian lines. One of the Prussians gave chase and opened fire. Woodhouse made believe that he had been hit, and his companion brought the machine down in a field. Immediately the Prussian, in one of the latest type battle planes, made his landing and went over to the other machine without bothering to cover the pilot with his revolver, Woodhouse meanwhile lying as if dead. Suddenly he leaped up, jammed his revolver under the Boche's nose and marched him over to the big battle plane, got in after him and with the gun against his ribs took him back to our lines, a prisoner. Later he returned and got the Prussian machine. Besides the machine there were some valuable papers taken, which proved very useful later.

In the Royal Naval Air Service, there is a young lieutenant, Murray Galbraith by name, with whom I once trained at the school at Dayton, Ohio. Murray is a great big fellow who gave up a splendid future—his father is one of the Canadian silver kings—to go into the flying service. He was sent to Dunkirk to do patrol work for one of the monitors lying off the coast. Over at Ostend the Prussians had made their staff headquarters in a certain hotel. Galbraith spotted this hotel and directed the shellfire of the monitor with such accuracy that the Prussian staff barely escaped annihilation.

On one of his flights over the Prussian lines he encountered five machines, one of which he disposed of. He got away from the rest and, coming on toward the Somme, ran into another group of Boches. Two of these he put out of business with a withering fire from his Lewis gun and then executed a loop and started earthward. His engine gave out, but he was just high enough to glide back over their lines and then to a point of safety near our lines.

When he landed his machine was literally shot to pieces. He received the D. S. O. for this and, I believe, has since been decorated again.

The Skill of British Airmen
By John Foster Fraser

Aviation, as yet in its infancy, has made its mark. In varied degrees, the construction and development of aircraft have been taken in hand by the countries of Europe, and by none more so than by Germany, which has spent enormous sums upon its bird-like Taube aeroplanes, as well as upon its fleet of Zeppelins. So important, indeed, is the latter type of airship regarded, that its inventor, Count Zeppelin, is one of the most intimate of the inner circle of the Kaiser's War Council. Despite all this, the operations in the air since war broke out have not been in the enemy's favour. In fact, Sir John French, Commander-in-Chief of the British Forces, has declared that the airmanship of the Royal Flying Corps has up to the present demonstrated its "personal ascendancy" over that of the enemy.

How daring some of the feats performed have been is shown by the raids made upon the enemy's headquarters at Düsseldorf. The official account of the first of them, a really brilliant piece of flying, stated that British aeroplanes of the naval wing delivered an attack on the Zeppelin shed. The conditions were rendered very difficult by the misty weather, but Flight-Lieutenant C. H. Collett dropped three bombs on the Zeppelin shed, approaching within four hundred feet. The extent of the damage done is not known. Flight-Lieutenant Collet's machine was struck by one projectile, but all the machines returned safely to their point of departure. The importance of this and similar incidents lies in the fact that they showed that measures of reprisal for German raids on unfortified towns could certainly be adopted, if desired, to almost any extent. The German official version of the affair by wireless said:

> One of the enemy's aeroplanes dropped bombs near Düsseldorf airship shed, but no damage was done.

But there were details that required filling in in this account, if only because the feat was of first importance to us. So, the above may be supplemented by the account of an eyewitness who states that the raid was cleverly and neatly executed. The British Flying Squadron broke up into two divisions. Each division had attached to it Belgian troops in motorcars and on motorcycles, who made arrangements for landing places where the airmen could get supplies of petrol. The slight fog allowed the airmen to fly at a height of nine hundred feet without being seen from below. Unfortunately, the airmen who set out for Cologne were unable to attain their objective on account of the fog, and, from the same cause, had to return, steering by compass alone. The expedition to Düsseldorf was successful. The airmen were able to fly over the Zeppelin sheds, causing a great panic among the German guards. Bombs were dropped on these sheds, and all the projectiles went home.

To this it may be added—since airmen are not so well-known as their other brothers in warfare—that Lieutenant Collet, who was born in Calcutta, was to have piloted a Beardmore British waterplane in the 1914 round-Britain flight, which was postponed on account of the war. He had resigned his commission in the Flying Corps, and after the flight he was to have taken up a position in the new aerial department of Messrs. Beardmore, the shipbuilders; but on the outbreak of war he rejoined the Flying Corps. He is aged twenty-five.

Should there be any disposition to question the testimony of Sir John French as to the efficiency of British flying men, corroboration is forthcoming from German quarters. The event was after Mons, and it was the German officer in charge of the Taube engaged in the affair who told the story. There is therefore no need to find excuse for quoting it just as related. Note should be taken of the state of terror into which the adventure apparently plunged him.

> I was instructed to do some important reconnoitring in the northern district of France, especially near Lille and Maubeuge. I left Belgium in my Taube biplane with a mechanic. While flying into France I suddenly heard the noise of an aeroplane, which I soon recognised as a British military Bristol biplane which had come to fight us. Our first tactics were to prevent the Bristol climbing higher than us, but the British machine was cleverly handled, and soon was 150 yards over us. Several attempts were made by us to fly higher, but the British aero-

plane checked them all. It was evident that each of us feared that the other would drop bombs on him. Meanwhile we had prudently turned northward, hoping to reach the German camp before the Englishman damaged us or forced us to land. The Bristol was coming closer and closer, and we felt like a bird on which a vulture was going to pounce.

I said to my mechanic: 'I think our last hour has come.' He answered with a laugh: 'Rather our last half-hour.' I am sure that if the Englishman had had any bombs aboard, I would not be here to tell the tale; but fortunately, he had none. He could not have missed us, as, owing to his clever steering, he was about fifty yards over us. These were terrible minutes. We fired our automatic revolvers at the enemy, and he responded vigorously. Our machine was hit several times, but not in vital parts. The wings show many revolver bullet holes.

We were nearing the Belgian boundary when I saw a small Bleriot monoplane come to the aid of the Bristol. The French aircraft reached 1,000 feet in no time, and then began flying in concentric circles around us, always drawing nearer, and the three machines engaged in an unprecedented duel, the occupants firing revolvers continually. Our ammunition was nearly exhausted when we heard energetic firing beneath. We had reached a German camp, where our terrible situation was speedily realised, and our soldiers were firing on the two enemy flying machines in order to cover our retreat and descent. We were saved, but, needless to say, I did no reconnoitring work that day.

That story of British daring and German fear needs no embellishment.

The following feat of a Blyth airman is noteworthy for its cool pluck. He was sent to accompany an officer on an army biplane, and went over the German lines at an altitude of 1,200 feet. They were met by a shower of bullets. Several struck the machine, but did no material damage until a shot struck the engine, knocking it out of service. By clever volplaning, however, the airmen succeeded in landing about two miles from the Allies' lines. A heavy fall on rough ground resulted in the Blyth man having his collar bone broken and a leg injured. The officer was injured about the face. As a party of Germans were hurrying towards them, they released the petrol, set fire to the machine, and decamped. They had many narrow escapes from capture, and the Blyth man's injuries became so painful that the officer had to carry him. He was placed in hospital, when the Germans shelled it and caused a precipitate removal. Two other hospitals being full, he was sent home.

What was described as the most thrilling story he had ever listened to was related to a *Times* correspondent at Havre by an eye-witness of an aeroplane duel between British and German aviators. It concerned a German aeroplane, flying high, which visited the British lines with the object of reconnoitring. As the machine hovered overhead, well out of reach of fire, a British airman shot up to the attack. The German saw his adversary, and attempted to attack him from above. Shots were fired, but they missed their mark. The British plane swept in a wide semicircle around the adversary, mounting steadily. The German tried to swoop in order to open fire at close range from above. A sudden giddy manoeuvring of both machines. Shots!

Another swift change of position, German and Britisher almost at the same altitude, but out of range of one another, and each fighting for the higher place. A rushing together, the two machines far up now, looking exactly like great birds in combat. . . . The distant sound of shooting. . . . Then a great struggle up and down, a darting hither and thither, each airman determined to win the advantage over his foe. . . . . . The machines advance and retire. . . . Suddenly the Britisher swings above. . . . The German reels and seems to stagger . . . and then, travelling more slowly than sight, the sound of shots. The German descends slowly to the ground. He is wounded. Victory was with the British flier.

In one case, at least, a British aviator did not come off the better in an encounter. The reason for this was that he was matched against two men who were in the enemy's machine. He had been particularly active in annoying the enemy by dropping bombs on them at various spots, with what damage, however, could not be ascertained.

Being alone on a single-seater monoplane, he was not able to use a rifle, and while circling above a German two-seater in an endeavour to get within pistol-shot, he was hit by the observer of the latter, who was armed with a rifle. He managed to fly back over our lines, and by great good luck he descended close to a motor ambulance, which at once conveyed him to hospital.

Viewed from the standpoint of an overhead thrill, the act of a British artificer, who executed repairs by fixing new blades to an air-ship while in the air, stands supreme in daring. The machine was returning from scouting operations when a propeller broke, and, crumpling up, dashed against the envelope. It was at once feared that all was over. But by a miracle the steel propeller did not break the envelope, although it shook the ship from stem to stern, throwing the crew to the floor of their cabin. But no sooner were the crew clear of one disaster than a worse one seemed imminent. For the ship was carried by a strong wind towards German territory.

It was seen that the only hope was to affix another propeller. So an engine-room artificer found a spare one, and there—2,500 ft. in the air!—clambered along the 2½-in. thick stanchion, and calmly set to work to fix the new blades. With practically no hold, seated on a "gas-pipe," 15 ft. from the cabin, this brave fellow worked for two and a half hours, not leaving his job until he had made certain of the soundness of his work. But the strain was terrific, and on returning to the cabin he almost collapsed in the arms of his comrades. For his brave conduct, he has been recommended for promotion.

What it feels like to be above fire and under fire was racily described by a member of the Royal Flying Corps, who, like so many other aviators, has experienced his baptism at the hands of the Germans, and, singular to relate, also at those of our friends, the French and Belgians. These particular experiences are contained in letters sent home by the aviator which appeared in the *Daily Mail*, and are instructive as showing the dangers to which airmen are exposed, together with the nerve and skill required in facing them.

The aviator had just come back from a reconnaissance of about 120 miles, he says:

> I got absolutely frozen, but I am getting used to that now. Besides, it's all in the day's work. It wasn't quite such an interesting reconnaissance as usual. We dropped one or two bombs on some bivouacs that must have stirred them up a bit, because they began firing at us with rifles. We only got hit once; but, then, the machine we were in is rather hard to hit, because its speed is something like eighty miles an hour.
> The Germans have some special guns for dealing with aircraft. They consist of a gun which fires a kind of shrapnel shell which bursts at a certain height. As soon as they find your height, they let off their shells, about seven or eight at a time, which burst all around you. Each shell is loaded with round bullets about the

size of a marble, and these shoot about when the shell explodes. Whenever we go up we have these antiaircraft guns popping off at us. We have nicknamed one of them 'Archibald.' He has a very distinctive way of firing at you. He'll let off one, just to see where it bursts, to find out his range by it, and then let off six—one after another. We take them more or less as a joke, but I think they are pretty sure to bring one of us down sooner or later. It is really only a matter of time.

Did I tell you of my first reconnaissance? It was at Maubeuge. I started off to fly over by Mons and Enghien and Ath—in that direction. We ran into clouds just beyond Mons, so had to turn back. As we were coming back over the French lines I saw a movement and bustle among the troops, and then there was the noise of about 1,000 rifles cracking at us. They had mistaken me for a German because my machine was different from most of the others! That was my baptism of fire, and I shall never forget it. My first sensations were those of surprise, which rapidly developed into a kind of fear, which, in turn, changed to fascination.

It positively fascinated me to see the holes appearing in the planes as each bullet ripped its way through (although there were only a few of them). I was looking at my instrument board to see what height I was, when suddenly a bullet hit the board and a splinter jumped up in front of me. At the same time a bullet pierced the petrol tank, and all the petrol ran out. Another one hit one of the instruments, and smashed it. When the petrol ran out, there was nothing for it but to come down, so I trusted to luck and came down in the first good field I saw. A dozen or so Belgian and French soldiers rushed out, apparently not sure whether I was English or German till I shouted, '*Anglais! Anglais!*' Then they bustled to and did all they could for me.

I happened to have two tanks, so I filled up the other one and got ready to start off again. The odd part of it was shrapnel began bursting in the field next to us, one after another, which seemed to point to the fact that Germans had brought me down, and not the French as I had supposed. A French major came up in a car and entreated me to hurry away. '*Vite, vite,*' he said. '*Les Allemands ne sont pas loin—trois kilomètres!*' ('Quick, quick. The Germans are not far away—about two miles!') I didn't believe him, but all the same I got into the machine. My passenger thought we should not be able to get out of the field, but we just managed it. Just before we started someone came up and said that an English girl would like to see me before we went, so I went into the middle of the crowd and found the girl (who turned out to be an American).

She said she had lived there (the name of the place was Solve-sur-Sambre, on the east of Maubeuge) for five years, and after blessing me (!) caught hold of my hand and wished me good luck. Just as we left the ground we were hit again; this time it hit the machine. It was altogether a most exciting afternoon. When we got back I counted twelve hits. Considering we were so low, they certainly ought to have done better than that!

A private in the Duke of Cornwall's Light Infantry relates one incident which struck him as being "quite exciting." He said that a German aeroplane came over the Allies' lines, and a French aeroplane headed it right off, while our guns commenced operations at the same time. The pompoms were going "*bang-bang*" all the while, and several British big guns had a pop at him, but he managed to get back to his own lines safely. In the same way, our aircraft were reconnoitring over the German positions. A British aviator had been over their lines and was coming back, when between thirty and forty shells were fired at him by the German guns; but not one of them hit him, although they were bursting all around.

In another case an English pilot, on emerging from a cloud, found immediately underneath him a German aeroplane. Swooping down to within revolver-shot, he emptied all his chambers, with an effect he could not observe, because the cloud once more enveloped him. Later on, when he emerged from the cloud again, he saw a small crowd gathered round a smashed aeroplane, and he came to the conclusion that his revolver-shots had had effect.

This is how an officer of the Royal Field Artillery tersely described an episode:

> The best effort of the lot is that performed by one of the Royal Flying Corps. He had engine trouble, and had to land in the German lines. Near his landing spot he found five German officers in a car. He kept 'em away with a rifle while his pilot repaired the engine. They then escaped by air.

Airmen in the Deserts of Egypt

Adventures of the Royal Flying Corps in Sinai
Told by F. W. Martindale

The land has its perils for the aviator, and so has the sea; but our "fliers" in Egypt have learnt to dread the treacherous desert more than anything else. Here are two little stories from the annals of the R. F. C.—one near tragedy, the other real tragedy, lightened only by the amazing self-sacrifice of a young officer and the dogged pluck of his mechanic, who posted up his diary while awaiting death. Recorded in the *Wide World Magazine*.

1—Flying Over the Ancient Holy Lands

Whatever the professional distinction may be between the two branches of the aviation service, the broad difference in the public mind between the Royal Flying Corps and the Royal Naval Air Service is that the former fly over land and the latter over sea. And whatever the relative advantages, and the reverse, of these opposite conditions may be, a certain amount of sympathy inevitably goes out to the naval airman in the supposedly more difficult element from which he starts and on which he has to make his "landing" on return. The mystery and the menace of the sea, which has always made sailors a race apart, is so real and apprehensible a thing, even to the landsman, that instinctively the sea is felt to be a source of greater peril to the airman than the land.

Be this as it may, it has fallen to the lot of the Royal Flying Corps in this war to face an "element"—if one may call it such—as mysterious as the ocean, and not a whit less menacing. This is the desert—a thing which casts a spell upon those who have to dare it as potent and as fearful as any with which the sea holds the mariner in thrall.

Mutable to the eye as the face of the waters, sudden and fickle in mood as the sea itself, there lurks in the desert an even grimmer menace than that which gives the sailor his wary, vigilant eye. The cruelty of the sea is nothing to the cruelty of the desert. Ask the airman who has made trial of both, and he will tell you that better a hundred times the risk of falling into the clutches of the uncertain sea than the chance of finding himself at the mercy of the pitiless desert.

Here is a case in point—a little excerpt from the doings of the Royal Flying Corps, which it would be hard to match even in the records of that adventurous service. Pilot and observer set off in an aeroplane upon a singlehanded reconnaissance towards the enemy's lines in Sinai. A long flight was made over the desert, and the machine was a long way from its base when that terrible bugbear known as "engine-trouble" developed. All attempts to right it in the air proved abortive, and a forced descent was made. The aeroplane alighted on the desert waste, and the two occupants worked feverishly to adjust the faulty mechanism. Their dismay can be imagined when they found repair impossible, and realised that between themselves and the Canal lay a stretch of some twenty miles of desert, over which no means of progress was possible to them save their own legs.

It says much for the loyalty to duty of these two airmen that they carefully dismantled the gun which was mounted on their machine before setting fire to the latter, and that they actually set off on their long tramp across the burning desert carrying the gun between them.

It soon became evident that any idea of saving the gun by taking it all the way with them was hopeless. The weight, not inconsiderable under any condition, was insupportable, and before long there was no course possible but to bury the weapon in the sand, obliterating as best they could all tell-tale traces which might reveal its hidden presence to a chance enemy patrol.

2—Over the Burning Desert with a Gun

Progress was easier when the cumbersome weapon had been disposed of. But it was not long before clothing had to be jettisoned also. The relatively thick and heavy garments of an aviator were intolerable under the savage rays of the sun, and one by one they had to be discarded. Even so, the going was terribly difficult and the journey most exacting. By means of a compass a direction due west was maintained, the one hope of the castaways being to keep on until some point on the Canal should be reached.

The hours went slowly by as mile after mile was laboriously covered. The strength of both men was steadily declining, but it was not until something more than half the estimated distance from their goal had been accomplished that either gave way. Then one collapsed; he could go no farther, he declared. His companion, well aware how fatally seductive a "rest" would inevitably be, bade him keep going, but without effect. The weary man's legs gave way beneath him; he sank down on the sand, and declared that he *preferred* to stay there rather than attempt to struggle on any longer.

Advice, persuasion, cajolery, threats, and even force were of no avail, and nothing remained but for the second man to continue the journey, with waning hope, alone. To stay with his comrade meant that both must inevitably perish miserably; by pressing on there was, at all events, a faint chance, not only of reaching the Canal himself, but of summoning aid to return in time to rescue the other.

For some miles the wretched survivor, now tortured by an awful thirst and so weakened that he seemed scarcely able to move his legs, staggered blindly on across the desert. He had consciousness enough to maintain his westerly direction, but as to how long he continued stumbling forward in this almost aimless fashion, or what distance he covered, he can hazard only the wildest guess. His progress became largely automatic. Force of will kept him moving, his reluctant limbs relapsing into semi-mechanical action.

At the moment of his direst extremity, as it seemed, when from sheer lack of power his body threatened to collapse altogether, the hapless wanderer espied a horse before him in the desert!

Now, if this were fiction, no writer, however cynical, would ever dare to introduce a horse at such a point of the narrative. The thing would be too absurd; the long arm of coincidence never reached so far as that! Nobody could be expected to believe it.

Yet the fact is as stated. At the psychological moment, when every new step taken might have proved his last, the wanderer saw before him in the desert the miraculous apparition of a horse. It can be easily supposed that at first, he did not believe his eyes. In his half-demented state, he feared the creature must be an hallucination—some trick of mirage, or the mere figment of his disordered brain. Only when he came nearer, and could hear as well as see the animal move, did a full realization of his good fortune begin to dawn upon him.

3—Tale of Modern Arabian Nights

A sail in unfrequented latitudes never seemed more truly a godsend to castaways at sea than this marvellous horse to the exhausted airman. It was but a stray animal belonging to some mounted unit which had drawn the peg of its head-rope and escaped from the horse-lines into the open desert, but to the incredulous eyes which suddenly perceived its presence it might well have been the famous magic steed of the Arabian Nights.

To catch the animal was the immediate thing to be done, and anyone who has tried to catch a shy horse in a paddock can imagine the hideous anxiety on the part of an exhausted man in approaching an animal which has the illimitable desert to manoeuvre in, and has but to kick up its heels to vanish in a trice over the horizon. Fortunately, the creature evinced but little shyness, and suffered itself to be taken without difficulty. It is probable, indeed, that this desert encounter was not less welcome on the one side than on the other.

One wonders how the would-be rider ever managed to get astride his lucky steed. His legs had little enough capacity for a spring left in them. But necessity and hope in combination provide a wonderful incentive and spur, and somehow or other he scrambled up. He himself has hazy recollections only of this stage of his adventures, and beyond the fact that he did mount that horse, and manage to set it going in a westerly direction, his recollections are vague.

The next phase of the story is contained in the narrative of the officer commanding a patrol vessel on the Suez Canal, who relates that while on duty his attention was directed to a strange figure riding on horseback along the eastern bank of the Canal. At first sight, he supposed it to be some mounted Arab or other nomad of the desert, but on closer inspection the horse did not seem to be of native type, and the rider's garb appeared unusual. On nearer approach the strange apparition resolved itself into a white man, of wild and haggard demeanour, dressed in a torn shirt and very little else, who bestrode bare-backed a troop-horse in distressed condition. Hailed by the patrol boat, the white horseman replied in English, and explained intelligibly, if a trifle incoherently, that he had come out of the desert, that his chum was lying some miles back in dire distress, if not already dead, and would somebody please hurry up and do something.

The conclusion of the story can be told in a sentence. A relief party was sent at once into the desert, the second airman was picked up exhausted but still alive, and at the date when the present writer last heard of them both parties of this strange adventure of the desert were little, if any, the worse for their experiences. As to the gallant troop-horse which played the part of a kind of *equus ex machina*, no peg in all the lines is now more firmly and securely driven in than his!

The story just related ends happily for all concerned; let me deal now with the reverse side of the shield!

4—Shot Himself in Self-Sacrifice

About the middle of June last year Second-Lieutenant Stewart Gordon Ridley, of the R.F.C., went out alone in his machine as escort to another pilot, who had with him a pilot named J. A. Garside. "Engine trouble" developed when Lieutenant Ridley had been flying for an hour and a half, and, as they could not put the matter right immediately on alighting, they decided to camp where they were for the night.

Next morning, as Ridley's engine still proved obdurate, the second pilot decided to fly back alone to the base, and return on the following day to the assistance of the two men. This programme was duly carried out, but when he got back the pilot found that Ridley and Garside, with the machine, had disappeared. A search party was immediately organized to scour the desert, and on the Sunday tracks were discovered. It was not until the Tuesday, however, that the missing 'plane was discovered. Beside it lay the dead bodies of Lieutenant Ridley and Garside. A diary was found on the mechanic, and the brief entries therein tell the tragic story of those last hours better than pages of description. The diary reads as follows:—

> *Friday.*—Mr. Gardiner left for Meheriq, and said he would come and pick one of us up. After he went we tried to get the machine going, and succeeded in flying for about twenty-five minutes. Engine then gave out. We tinkered engine up again, succeeded in flying about five miles next day (Saturday), but engine ran short of petrol.
>
> *Sunday.*—After trying to get engine started, but could not manage it owing to weakness—water running short, only half a bottle—Mr. Ridley suggested walking up to the hills. Six p.m. (Sunday): Found it was farther than we thought; got there eventually; very done up. No luck. Walked back; hardly any water—about a spoonful. Mr. Ridley shot himself at ten-thirty on Sunday whilst my back was turned. No water all day; don't know how to go on; got one Verey light; dozed all day, feeling very weak; wish someone would come; cannot last much longer.

Monday.—Thought of water in compass, got half bottle; seems to be some kind of spirit. Can last another day. Fired Lewis gun, about four rounds; shall fire my Verey light tonight; last hope without machine comes. Could last days if I had water.

The captain of the Imperial Camel Corps, with which the aviators were co-operating, formed the opinion that Lieutenant Ridley shot himself in the hope of saving the mechanic, the water they had being insufficient to last the two of them till help arrived. The commanding officer of the R. F. C. states:

There is no doubt in my mind that he performed this act of self-sacrifice in the hope of saving the other man.

The history of the R. F. C is a short one, but it is already full of glorious deeds.

Deeds of Heroism and Daring
Albert Bushnell Hart

One of the Great "Aces"
Raoul Lufbery, the Connecticut Boy Who Roamed the World to Die a Hero in France

The Great War brought into bold relief no more romantic figure or daring spirit than that of Major Raoul Lufbery, from Wallingford, Conn. The bare facts of his life have the flavour of incidents taken from the adventure story of a highly imaginative fiction writer. There is no need of invention or added colour to make his history a thrilling tale. No presentation of it, however bald and commonplace the narrative, can cheat it of its romance and heroism. That he was one of the chief of the American "Aces" is in itself an epitome of adventure that might easily be elaborated into a volume.

Lufbery was an adventurer in the dashing sense of the word. His blood was filled with the essence of unrest, the energy of motion that would not let him stay fixed to place. When he was seventeen years old Wallingford held him too much cabined and confined. He ran away from home as an explorer of the unknown world. Drawn, perhaps, by the spell of ancestral affinities, he made his way to France and wandered from place to place in the land of legend and romance, working at any job that would provide his keep and supply him with funds for his next excursion.

From France he sailed to Algiers, where he remained till he had satisfied his interest, when he set off for other scenes—Egypt, the Balkans, Germany, South America and then back to Wallingford for a peep at the home folks. He chuckled appreciatively on learning that his father was off doing a bit of globe-vagabonding on his own account.

Major Raoul Lufbery, an American, Who Was Loved by Fellow-Flyers

He stopped at home for a year, when the wander-bubbles of his blood got into ferment again, and trotting down to New Orleans he was tempted by military possibilities and enlisted in the Regular Army. He was sent to the Philippines, where he displayed such proficiency as rifleman that he won all the regimental prizes for the best marksmanship.

That skill in getting bullets into the right spot was one of his great assets when he came to battling in the air over the fields of France.

But even the army waxed tame for Lufbery, and when his term of enlistment expired he was ready and eager to nose out what the still strange parts of the world had to offer him. He sailed for Japan, sampled the beauties and novelties of that country and then dipped into China. From China, he went into India. A characteristic anecdote is told of him as ticket-seller in one of the railway stations of India. It has been said that he sustained himself with any kind of odd job as he roamed the world, and ticket-selling was one of the tedious sort of occupations least to his liking. A pompous type of native one day stood at the wicket.

"Want a ticket?" Lufbery asked.

"Say 'Sir' when you speak to me," said the native, loftily.

The Price of a Job

With never a wink, Lufbery left his place, approached the offended person, took him by the back of the neck and with neatness and dispatch ejected him from the station. Under English civil law one is promptly summoned for assault, and as the person Lufbery had treated so summarily in accord with his own ideas of fitness chanced to be the richest and most influential merchant of Bombay, the summons cost the ticket-seller his place. Cochin-China was his resort, Saigon his haven, and there, if you please, he viewed with envious admiration the aerial antics of Marc Pourpe, the famous trick flyer.

There came a day when Pourpe lost his mechanic, and his exhibitions came to a stop while he made vain quest among the natives for a substitute. None cared for the office, preferring infinitely the understood foundation of Mother Earth to antics in the air. Quite right—Lufbery applied for the job. Was he a mechanic? No. Did he know anything about an aeroplane motor? Not a thing.

"Why the deuce, then, do you come bothering me?" demanded the irritated Pourpe.

"I don't know the job now," Lufbery said, "but I can learn. You only have to show me once. Take me on. You won't regret it. I'm not afraid of work."

Marc Pourpe is quoted as saying to some friends later in relating the incident:

> His reasoning was full of logic. His method was original. I agreed, and I will say that never have I seen a person more devoted, more intelligent and more useful. He is already better informed about a motor than most of the so-called mechanics of Paris. Moreover, this boy has hung his hat in every country in the world. He is not a man, he is an encyclopaedia. He can tell you what the weather is in a given season in Japan, in Egypt, in America, or in France. He observes everything and once he has noticed it, it is engraved on his memory.
>
> He told me that in all his travels he had never been more than a week without working. He was hospital interne at Cairo, a stevedore in Calcutta, station master in India, a soldier in America. I am glad he is now a mechanic.
>
> If he likes it, I will take him back with me at the end of my tour and will keep him with me. It is rare to find a good mechanic. His name is Raoul Lafberg, and he spent his childhood in the vicinity of Bourges. If I return with him, you will see what a sympathetic character chance has thrown in my way. So once more in my life everything goes well."

This shift of name on the sudden from Lufbery to Lafberg was due to a hope that the Frenchified turn would the more favourably determine Pourpe to engage his services, especially as Lufbery spoke French fluently, having learned it in his three years' stay in France.

Joins the Foreign Legion

So, it was that Lufbery, as Pourpe's mechanic, found himself in France when the war storm burst. Pourpe, who had a new type of plane, promptly enlisted as a flyer for his beloved France. As an American Lufbery could not be accepted except as a member of the Foreign Legion, which he hastened to join in the expectation that he could be transferred thence to service with his friend, which was done. But they were not long together at the front. Pourpe was killed the first or second of December, 1914.

Thereupon Lufbery applied for admission to the regular French air service which was granted and in a short time he was on the front with the Escadrille of bombardment, V. 102.

But it was not until he joined the newly organized Escadrille Lafayette that his career of distinction began. His first victim was brought down, over Etain, July 30, 1916, the second five days later. He was cited by the French Government thus:

> A model of address, of coolness, of courage. He has distinguished himself by numerous long distance bombardments and by the daily combats he has had with enemy aeroplanes. On July 30, he unhesitatingly attacked at close range four enemy machines. He shot one of them down near our own lines. He successfully brought down a second on the 4th of August, 1916.

His record grew apace. He got his third August 8, his fourth August 12, his fifth October 12, and became an "Ace." In December, he brought down two in one day after a fight that nearly cost him his life as his jacket was torn with bullets. That victory gained him the award of the Legion of Honour. Incidentally, he was the first American to receive from England the British Military Cross which was conferred on him June 12, 1917, when his record had mounted to ten enemy planes.

That tenth plane exploit, by the way, was memorable. Lufbery was alone at an altitude of 18,000 feet when, at a distance, he saw a formation of seven Boche machines. Two of them were two-seater observation machines, the others were the protective escort. He flew into the sun to wait for a chance to attack. Soon one of the seven cut loose from the others, and immediately Lufbery dived for it and began firing, taking the enemy by surprise. After thirty shots or so his gun jammed, but no more shots were necessary. The enemy machine wobbled, shifted and began its downward plunge, and as Lufbery volplaned away he saw the wrecked machine crash into the German trenches.

In an article written for the French publication *La Guerre Aérienne*, Lufbery describes an encounter he had one day when he was sent scouting over the Vosges, the panoramic beauty of which had so enthralled him he flew in sheer delight of the vision, nevertheless "all the time on guard."

Suddenly an enemy appeared a little below and behind him. He wrote:

> It is a little one-seater biplane of the *Fokker* or *Halberstadt* type. A glance around assures me that he is alone. I am surprised at this, for it is certainly the first time that a machine of this sort has deliberately placed itself in a position so disadvantageous

for fighting. Perhaps it is a trap. One never knows! If it only may prove to be a beginner, lacking experience, who listens to nothing but his courage in his purpose to become one of the great Aces of his country.

Attacks a Master of His Art

However, that may be, the wind keeps blowing from the west and carries me farther and farther into the lines. It will not do to allow the Boche to have this advantage too long: I decide to begin the attack without losing another second.

An about face, followed by a sudden double spin, carries me a little behind my adversary. Profiting by this advantage I dive upon him, but with a remarkable skill he gets out of range of my machine gun. He has anticipated my manoeuvre and parried the blow before it was struck. I am now aware that I have to do with a master of his art. This first encounter has proved it to me.

Making my machine tango from right to left, I saw him again below me but much nearer than before by at least forty yards.

Suddenly he noses up as if to begin a looping, and in this awkward position fires a volley at me which I dodge by a half turn to the right. A second time I attack but with no more success. The wind carries us to the north of Mulhouse, and I begin to ask myself if I am not playing my adversary's game for him in delaying longer.

At this moment, I chanced to glance in the direction of Belfort, which was about twelve miles within our lines. I perceived in the air little white flakes. Evidence of the presence of a Boche. A lucky chance! I had now an excuse for abandoning without loss of honour the match, which I confess I am not at all sorry to leave. Only before leaving my adversary I feel that I must show him that I appreciate that he is a valiant foe and respect him as such. Drawing my left arm out of the fuselage I wave him a sign of *adieu*. He understands and desires to show courtesy on his part, for he returns my farewell.

All my attention is turned toward him whom I already consider as my new prey, a big white two-seater of very substantial appearance.

I draw nearer and nearer to him. Good luck! For the first time since I have been a chaser I am going to have the good fortune to battle within our lines. Also, this increases my confidence until it makes me disregard measures of caution, even the science of tactics.

Another motive impels me to take more than ordinary risks. I am determined that he shall not escape me, and I make up my mind to shoot at him until I have won the victory.

What joy if I can only lodge a ball in his motor, or in his gasoline tank, which would oblige him to make a landing on French soil! Then I should be able to speak with the conquered and ask them their impressions of the aerial duel in which they had just taken part. But there is an old French proverb which says '*You must not sell the skin of the bear before you have killed him.*' I had occasion that day to prove the wisdom of this as you shall soon see.

"Poor Coucou"

Enough of dreaming! The moment for action has arrived. Quickly I place myself in the rear and on the tail of my enemy from whom I am separated by a distance of about fifty yards. Then I open fire with my machine gun, and continue firing up to the moment when my plane, his superior in speed, arrives so near the big two-seater that a collision seems inevitable.

Quickly I pull up, leap over the obstacle, and fall in a glide on the right wing. Increasing my speed, I re-establish my equilibrium and prepare to tempt fortune a second time.

Curse the luck! It is of no use. The motor, the soul of my aeroplane, has received a mortal wound and is about to draw its last breath.

Turning my head, I discover that the ailerons are also seriously injured. My enemy fortunately does not seem to wish to profit by the situation. He continues his flight in the direction of his own lines. Perhaps I have wounded him very seriously. I hope so. Anyway, his flight leaves me master of the field. But that is a very small consolation. And also of short duration; for I am coming down faster and faster. At last I safely take the ground on the nearest flying field within gliding distance.

Pilots, observers, mechanics surround me and besiege me with questions. They have seen the fight and want the details. For the moment, I do not explain much but that I have encountered a Boche who does not understand joking! Besides, I was in a hurry to examine the wounds of my little aeroplane. It is very ill, poor thing! Three bullets in the motor, the gasoline tank ruined, a strut out of commission, many holes in the hood, finally the left aileron was cut and broken off by the bullets. It had made its last flight! Poor Coucou!

An admirable story of Lufbery in *Heroes of Aviation* says in conclusion:

> To recount all the aerial successes of this American champion is but to repeat the usual details of his sober inspection of his aeroplane and his arms before dawn; his calm scrutiny of the skies for the black crosses of the enemy planes; his adroit manoeuvring for the best position from which to surprise the foe; his determined and patient attack; his exactness in machine gun marksmanship; his jubilant return to his comrades with another certain victory on his score.
>
> During months of his service in France Lufbery suffered from acute seizures of rheumatism which frequently necessitated his return to the hospital. Quiet and unassuming in his conversation, Lufbery won universal respect from the mechanics and affectionate loyalty from his comrades. Everyone who met him felt as Marc Pourpe wrote, 'He is not a man, he is an encyclopaedia.'
>
> When America entered the war, and began her preparations for her own Air Service in France, certain of the experienced fighting pilots who had been fighting for France were given charge of the new American *escadrilles*. Lufbery and William Thaw, both original members of N. 124, the Escadrille Lafayette, were commissioned Majors. To them fell the task of organizing the eager youths who were to assist in clearing from the skies of France the invading Huns.
>
> Possessed of all the honours that his army could bestow upon a noble soldier, and wracked with physical pains that were daily increased by inclement weather, an ordinary man would have been satisfied to seek his ease and fill his required duties with the instructions to his pilots. But Major Lufbery instructed by example, not by speech. Not unmindful of his value to his comrades as their mentor and commander and impelled by an ardour that knew no rest, Lufbery continued his active patrolling, exposed himself to every risk.

The Last Flight

On Sunday, May 19th, the American Ace went aloft over Toul with his fighting squadron. Enemy fighting machines were flying over the American line. The latest designed *Fokker* aeroplane, a single-seater triplane, appeared deep enough within our territory to be cut off before he could escape. Lufbery darted swiftly to the attack.

Exact details of any air combat are known only to the combatants. Fighting machines of today, (1920), move with a speed of 140 miles per hour. Approaching each other they lessen the distance between them at the rate of over 400 feet each second. Let someone calculate the fraction of an instant given to the pilot in which he plans his manoeuvre, alters his position, takes his aim, and presses the trigger!

Lufbery's machine fell in flames. He was seen to jump from the blazing mass when 2,000 feet from the ground. A parachute attachment might have saved his life as his body was found to be uninjured from the enemy's fire. A non-inflammable fuel tank might have permitted him to continue his attack until the *Fokker* triplane dropped as his nineteenth victory.

Deprived of these improvements, Lufbery died. With his lamented loss, the title of the American Ace of Aces passed to Sergeant Frank L. Baylies, of New Bedford, Massachusetts, who after eight months at the front had amassed a total of twelve enemy machines. Upon the gallant death of Baylies, Lieutenant Putnam of Brookline, Massachusetts, with ten official victories, headed the American list of Aces.

Though officially credited with only eighteen planes brought down in single combat, Lufbery was, in fact, the victor over twice that number of enemy planes. The rule for official recognition requires that a fall must be attested by eyewitnesses in addition to the flyer. Many of Lufbery's "downs" were inside the enemy lines beyond the observation of any of his comrades, and others fell in such a way that it could not be said positively that they were destroyed.

The Lafayette Escadrille

An Air Squadron Made Famous by American Youth Before America Entered the War

In the first years of the war, when the war was yet a European War, when America as a nation was not ready to act, a group of American boys—roused by the righteousness of the war against Germany, and longing to help France—finally enlisted in the French aviation service. They had come to repay the debt America owed to the people who had sent Lafayette in her time of need. Therefore, their section was given the name of Lafayette Escadrille. Americans glory in the homage paid to the daring deeds of Kiffin Rockwell, Victor Chapman, Norman Prince and Jim McConnell, of Thaw, Lufbery, Hall, Masson and Cowdin. Jim McConnell wrote a little book called *Flying for France*, in which he describes with a vividness born of the gallant affection he felt for his friends and comrades the deeds of that glorious group, and the deaths of three of them. Then he too fell.

McConnell first joined the American ambulance service in the Vosges, and was mentioned several times for conspicuous bravery in saving wounded under fire. It was in the ambulance service that he won the *Croix de Guerre*.

Gradually, however, this heroism drew on a deeper feeling. The spirit of adventure gave way to the spirit of liberty. France's struggle took on a new aspect. McConnell gave up the ambulance service and enlisted in the French flying corps.

Immediately he began to feel something more than the mere bond of common danger drawing him to the members of the *Escadrille*. They were like brothers who had managed to grow up friends as well as kinsmen. They were a picked lot. There was William Thaw, of Pittsburg, the pioneer of them all; Norman Prince, of Boston; Elliot Cowdin, of New York; Bert Hall, of Texas, and his chum James Bach—the first to fall into German hands. Bach had smashed into a tree in going to the assistance of a companion who had broken down in landing a spy in the German lines. Both he and his French companion had been captured. The last of the original six was Didier Masson. Soon Lufbery came, and Kiffin Rockwell of Asheville, N. C., and Victor Chapman of New York. Rockwell and Chapman had both been wounded in other branches of the service.

It was Rockwell who brought down the *Escadrille's* first plane in his initial aerial combat.

> He was flying alone, when, over Thann, he came upon a German on reconnaissance. He dived and the German turned toward his own lines, opening fire from a long distance. Rockwell kept straight after him. Then, closing to within thirty yards, he

DISTINGUISHED AVIATORS OF THE LAFAYETTE ESCADRILLE.
From the left: Lufbery, Hinkle, Thenault, Bigelow, and Thaw.

pressed on the release of his machine gun, and saw the enemy gunner fall backward and the pilot crumple up sideways in his seat. The plane flopped downward and crashed to earth just behind the German trenches. Swooping close to the ground Rockwell saw its debris burning away brightly. He had turned the trick with but four shots and only one German bullet had struck his Nieuport.

The section was soon transferred to more dangerous territory. They were needed at Verdun. Fighting there came thick and fast, McConnell describes the activity of almost every one there. And every one was active.

> Hall brought down a German observation craft. Thaw dropped a Fokker in the morning, and on the afternoon of the same day there was a big combat far behind the German trenches. Thaw was wounded in the arm, and an explosive bullet detonating on Rockwell's wind-shield tore several gashes in his face. Despite the blood which was blinding him Rockwell managed to reach an aviation field and land. Thaw, whose wound bled profusely, landed in a dazed condition just within our lines. He was too weak to walk, and French soldiers carried him to a field dressing-station, whence he was sent to Paris for further treatment. Rockwell's wounds were less serious and he insisted on flying again almost immediately.

How Chapman Fought

A week or so later Chapman was wounded. Considering the number of fights, he had been in, and the courage with which he attacked it was a miracle he had not been hit before.

He always fought against odds and far within the enemy's country. He flew more than any of us, never missing an opportunity to go up, and never coming down until his gasoline was giving out. His machine was a sieve of patched-up bullet holes. His nerve was almost superhuman and his devotion to the cause for which he fought sublime. The day he was wounded he attacked four machines. Swooping down from behind, one of them, a *Fokker*, riddled Chapman's plane.

One bullet cut deep into his scalp, but Chapman, a master pilot, escaped from the trap, and fired several shots to show he was still safe. A stability control had been severed by a bullet. Chapman held the broken rod in one hand, managed his machine with the other, and succeeded in landing on a nearby aviation field. His wound was dressed, his machine repaired, and he immediately took the air in pursuit of some more enemies. He would take no rest, and with bandaged head continued to fly and fight.

Balsley, a newcomer, managed to get wounded in the meantime. He had started out with a party of four that had met a German squadron. Balsley attacked the nearest German:

> Only to receive an explosive bullet in his thigh. Extra cartridge rollers, dislodged from their case, hit his arms. He was tumbling straight toward the trenches, but by an effort he regained control, righted the plane, and landed without disaster.
>
> Soldiers carried him to shelter, and later he was taken to a field hospital, where he lingered for days between life and death. Ten fragments of the explosive bullet were removed from his stomach. He bore up bravely and became the favourite of the wounded officers in whose ward he lay.
>
> When we flew over to see him they would say: '*Il est un brave petit gars, l'aviateur américain.*' (He's a brave little fellow, the American aviator.) On a shelf by his bed, done up in a handkerchief, he kept the pieces of bullet taken out of him, and under them some sheets of paper on which he was trying to write to his mother, back in El Paso.
>
> Balsley was awarded the *Médaille Militaire* and the *Croix de Guerre*, but the honours scared him. He had seen them decorate officers in the ward before they died.

The First of Them to Die

Then came Chapman's last fight. Before leaving, he had put two bags of oranges in his machine to take to Balsley, who liked to suck them to relieve his terrible thirst, after the day's flying was over. There was an aerial struggle against odds, far within the German lines, and Chapman, to divert their fire from his comrades, engaged several enemy airmen at once. He sent one tumbling to earth, and had forced the others off when two more swooped down upon him.

The wings of his plane suddenly buckled and the machine dropped like a stone.

Chapman had only started the list of deaths. He was to be followed by perhaps the most beloved of all the section. Kiffin Rockwell had started off with Lufbery one morning. Just before he reached the lines he "spied a German machine under him flying at 11,000 feet." Rockwell had fought more combats than the rest of the *Escadrille* put together, says McConnell.

> He had shot down many German machines that had fallen in their lines, but this was the first time he had had an opportunity of bringing down a Boche in our territory.

Rockwell approached so close to the enemy plane that it seemed there would be a collision. The German aeroplane carried two machine guns. When Rockwell started his dive, the enemy opened a rapid fire.

> Rockwell plunged through the stream of lead and only when very close to his enemy did he begin shooting. For a moment, it looked as if the German was falling, but then the French machine turned rapidly nose down, the wings of one side broke off and fluttered in the wake of the airplane, which hurtled earthward in a rapid drop. It crashed into the ground in a small field—a field of flowers—a few hundred yards back of the trenches. It was not more than two and a half miles from the spot where Rockwell, in the month of May, brought down his first enemy machine. The Germans immediately opened up on the wreck with artillery fire. In spite of the bursting shrapnel, gunners from a nearby battery rushed out and recovered poor Rockwell's broken body.
> Lufbery engaged a German craft but before he could get to close range two *Fokkers* swooped down from behind and filled his aeroplane full of holes. Exhausting his ammunition, he landed at Fontaine, an aviation field near the lines. There he learned of Rockwell's death and was told that two other French machines had been brought down within the hour. He ordered his gasoline tank filled, procured a full band of cartridges and soared up into the air to avenge his comrade. He sped up and down the lines, and made a wide detour to Habsheim, where the Germans have an aviation field, but all to no avail. Not a Boche was in the air.

No greater blow could have befallen the *Escadrille* than Rockwell's

THE MARINES WATCH ON THE RHINE
General Neville decorating the Colours of the 6th Regiment with the *Croix de Guerre* at Coblenz, Germany.

death. "The bravest and best of us all is no more," said the French captain.

Jim McConnell writes:

> Kiffin was the soul of the *Escadrille*. "He was loved and looked up to by not only every man in our flying corps, but by everyone who knew him. Kiffin was imbued with the spirit of the cause for which he fought and gave his heart and soul to the performance of his duty. He said: 'I pay my part for Lafayette and Rochambeau,' and he gave the fullest measure. The old flame of chivalry burned brightly in this boy's fine and sensitive being. With his death France lost one of her most valuable pilots. When he was over the lines the Germans did not pass— and he was over them most of the time.
>
> Rockwell had been given the *Médaille Militaire* and the *Croix de Guerre*, on the ribbon of which he wore four palms, representing the four magnificent citations he had received in the order of the army.

Kiffin was given a funeral worthy of a general.

> His brother, Paul, who had fought in the Legion with him, and who had been rendered unfit for service by a wound, was granted permission to attend the obsequies. Pilots from all nearby camps flew over to render homage to Rockwell's remains. Every Frenchman in the aviation at Luxeuil marched behind the bier. The British pilots, followed by a detachment of five hundred of their men, were in line, and a battalion of French troops brought up the rear. As the slow-moving procession of blue and khaki-clad men passed from the church to the graveyard, airplanes circled at a feeble height above and showered down myriads of flowers.

The fates seemed to be envious of the American section in France. Rockwell had fallen September 23. On the 15th of October Norman Prince died. McConnell writes:

> It was hard to realise that poor old Norman had gone, but I do not think he minded going. He wanted to do his part before being killed, and he had more than done it.

Jim's Turn Came

Thus, did Jim McConnell—honest, tender, courageous Jim, Irish

A Few Members of the Lafayette Escadrille

Jim—glory in the glory of his friends and mourn their loss. His good humour and native wit remained to the last, but the deaths of those so dear to him were deepening his character. There are touches of tense seriousness in the book—a tragic note at times. It was hard to see those brave fellows go one by one, and so steadily. And you never could tell which of your remaining friends was to go next. Then of a sudden came Jim's turn. There are a few letters which describe Jim's death as tenderly as Jim wrote about Chapman and Rockwell and Prince. The affection, loyalty, and undying gallantry of the group is quite evident. In one of these letters, dated March 21, 1917, to Paul Rockwell, Edmond Genet tells of the last flight:

> On Monday morning, Mac, Parsons, and myself went out at nine o'clock on the third patrol of the *Escadrille*. We had orders to protect observation machines along the new lines around the region of Ham. Mac was leader, I came second and Parsons followed me. Before we had gone very far Parsons was forced to go back on account of motor trouble.
> Mac and I kept on, and up to ten o'clock were circling around the region of Ham, watching out for the heavier machines doing reconnoitring work below us. We went higher than a thousand meters. About ten, for some reason or other of his own, Mac suddenly headed into the German lines toward Saint Quentin—perhaps for observation purposes—and I naturally followed close to his rear and above him.
> At any rate, we had gotten north of Ham and quite inside the hostile lines, when I saw two Boche machines crossing toward us from the region of Saint Quentin at an altitude higher than ours—we were then about 1,600 meters up. I supposed Mac saw them too. One Boche was far ahead of the other, and was in position to dive at any moment on Mac. I saw the direction Mac was taking, and pulled back climbing up, in order to gain an advantageous height over the nearest Boche. It was cloudy and misty and I had to keep my eyes on him all the time, so naturally I lost track of Mac.

The letter goes on to tell how the writer got back—to find Mac had not returned.

> The one hope that we have is that some news of Mac will be brought by civilians who might have witnessed his flight over the lines north of Ham. We likewise hope that Mac was merely

forced to land inside the enemy lines on account of a badly damaged machine, or a bad wound, and is well, but a prisoner. I wish, Paul, that I had been able to help Mac during his combat. The mists were thick, and consequently seeing any distance was difficult. I would have gone out that afternoon to look for him, but my machine was so damaged it took until yesterday afternoon to be repaired. Lieutenant de Laage and Lufbery did go out with their Spads, around the region north of Ham, toward Saint Quentin, but saw nothing of a Nieuport grounded or anything else to give news of what had occurred.

Four days later Genet wrote:

The evening before last definite news was brought to us that a badly smashed Nieuport had been found by French troops. Beside it was the body of a sergeant-pilot which had been there at least three days and had been stripped of all identification papers, flying clothes and even the boots. They got the number of the machine, which proved without further question that it was poor Mac.

Mac has been buried right there beside the road, and we will see that the grave is decently marked with a cross. The captain brought back a square piece of canvas cut from one of the wings, and we are going to get a good picture we have of Mac enlarged and placed on this with a frame. I suppose that Thaw or Johnson will attend to his belongings which he had asked to be sent to you. In the letter which he had left in case of his death he concludes with the following words: 'Good luck to the rest of you. *Vive la France!*'

All honour to him, Paul. The world, as well as France, will look up to him just as it is looking up to your fine brother and the rest who have given their lives so freely and gladly for this big cause.

The captain has already put in a proposal for a citation for Mac, and also one for me. Mac surely deserved it, and lots more, too.

McConnell was awarded the *Croix de Guerre* with palm.

A "Legendary Hero"

The Place in Fame to Which the French Assign Their Miracle "Ace"

In that charming French style of which he is a known master,

Henry Bordeaux tells the story of a frail little boy, delicate as a girl and having the general appearance of one, with his long curls, his too pretty face, his pale complexion, his gentle manners. Because he was so frail of body and so uncertain of health he was closely looked after by the women of the household, which means, among other things, that he was quite thoroughly spoiled. The child looked like a little princess, as though adapted more to a future of effeminate surroundings, not like a boy in whose infant breast waited a great spirit.

One day, when the child was about six years old, it suddenly occurred to the father that they were taking a wrong course with the boy. After reflection, he took the boy on his knee and said to him:

"I've a great mind to take you with me where I am going."

"Where are you going, papa?"

"Where I am going only men go."

"I wish to go with you."

The father hesitated, but finally said:

"After all, it is better to be too soon than too late. Get your hat. I'll take you."

He took him to the hair-cutter's.

"I'm going to have my hair cut," said the father. "How about yours?"

"I wish to do as the men do," the boy answered. And the beautiful curls were shorn.

There were tears when the mother folded her transformed darling to her breast, but the child stiffening proudly declared: "*Je suis un homme!*"

Bordeaux says here:

"*Il sera un homme, mais il restera longtemps un gamin aussi. Longtemps? Preque jusqu'à la fin—à ses heurs, jusqu'à la fin.*"

It was Georges Guynemer, who not so very long after flamed out a boy hero of France, doing deeds that struck the world with wonderment, and while the world marvelled vanished mysteriously, leaving no trace behind.

Small and feminine, educated chiefly by governesses and his sisters, later a day student at the Lyceum, afterwards for a time at Stanislas, he was not the stuff for a soldier, yet soldier he wished to be when France set out to repel the German horde. He was twenty years old then. He hastened to his father.

"I'm going to enlist."

"You are in luck."

"Ah! you authorise me!"

"I envy you."

"Then as an old soldier you can help me. You can speak for me."

"I will."

But it was to no avail. He was not able to carry the equipment and endure the fatigue of a private, and the effects of a childhood's illness made it impossible for him to serve in the cavalry. He was rejected—laughed at by some, be it said.

He made a second attempt to enlist with no better result. Says M. Bordeaux:

"He returned with his father to Biaritz, pale, silent, mournful, in such a state of rage and bitterness that his face was distorted." He wrote to his old preceptor at Stanislas:

"If I have to lie at the bottom of an auto-camion I wish to go to the front; and I will go. I mean to serve, it doesn't matter where nor how, it doesn't matter in what branch, but go to the front, serve I will."

That sort of spirit is not to be denied. Fate and circumstances make way for it.

He met the pilot of an airplane one day and in conversation with him asked: "How can one get into the air service?"

"See the captain; you'll find him at Pau."

A Small Beginning

His parents, or rather his father, consenting, he was on his way to Pau next morning. He rushed to Captain Bernard-Thierry with his plea. The captain objected. Georges pleaded, passionately, tearfully, begging even as a child for a desired object. The troubled captain made the only practicable concession—he would receive the youth as a mechanician student. The heavens opened. "That's the thing! That's the thing! I know automobiles." And so, it began, with hard work to the like of which he had never been accustomed, his endurance of which was problematical. But January 26, 1915, he was named as pilot student; March 10, 1915, he made his veritable first flight. In a letter to his father about this time he said:

> I believe I am not making a reputation for prudence, but I hope this will come. I shall know soon.

That reputation never came, on the contrary it was said of him:

> Returning almost daily from his chases with his aeroplane and often his clothing riddled with bullets, hurling himself with

CAPTAIN GUYNEMER,
France's immortal knight of the air.

absolute abandon against three, ten, fifteen or twenty enemy machines in formation, among which he usually succeeded in bringing down one or more; exulting in the number of wounds which his faithful planes brought home as if to bear witness to his charmed life, and encircling them with red paint to make them more conspicuous; on two occasions shooting down an enemy plane with a single bullet; on May 25, 1917, bringing down four enemy aeroplanes in one day—these extraordinary exploits coupled with the very extraordinary energy of this slim boy soon placed him upon a pedestal which raised him high above his comrades; and by reason of his many miraculous escapes from certain death, eventually surrounded him with a halo of fame unknown to the French populace since the day of Jeanne d'Arc.

Conqueror in fifty-three aerial combats wherein the result was officially established by the verification of three or more eyewitnesses, Guynemer brought down as many more German aeroplanes quite as effectively if less officially. His comrades in the *escadrille* knew this and respected their chief accordingly.

Possessed of every decoration that a grateful nation could officially bestow upon him, conscious of a position in the public esteem that, tinctured as it was with the legendary, illumined him with more glory and worship than was accorded even to a Joffre or a Foch, Georges Guynemer fulfilled the expectations of his fellow countrymen, when on September 11, 1917, he disappeared from the eyes of the world while in the full exercise of his duty.

The heavens swallowed him up, and to this day no reliable clue to his disappearance has been discovered. Small wonder then that the people of France in contemplation of this last exploit of their adored hero place his memory with one acclaim alongside the niche so long occupied by the heroic Jeanne d'Arc!

MIRACULOUS ESCAPES

His fellows and the soldiers in general were devoted to him; and that their devotion was something profounder than lip-service one incident of his career, one of his narrow escapes, will attest. It was in September, 1916. He was far within the enemy lines combating seven machines when a shot penetrated the radiator of his engine and the motor stopped. He was then quite fifteen miles distant from his own

A Duel Above the Clouds
A German plane falling in flames after a fight with a French plane.

lines and about twelve thousand feet in the air. There was nothing for it but to point his machine for home, with the least practicable slant, and trust to the glide sustaining him until he could reach home lines. The turn made, he gave all his attention to his pursuers, who, not suspecting his plight and having a lively respect for the generalship of the redoubtable "Ace," seemed to think discretion the better part of valour, did not continue the chase but dived for their own quarters. The machine on its glide fell lower and lower as he approached the trenches and finally the German gunners recognised the craft as that of the dreaded young champion and the guns were levelled at him, and he was gliding through a veritable shower of bursting shrapnel. His machine was riddled and it was a grave question if it could reach the French lines. It crossed the German trenches a scant fifty feet above the heads of the enemy who stood up in the trenches in their eagerness to send a shot into the tattered plane that would bring it down.

The French soldiers, who had watched the coming of the *Cigogne* through the rain of bullets and realised the helplessness of their idol, were recklessly and excitedly hanging over their trenches raging that they were powerless to help. Almost simultaneously with Guynemer's consciousness of his inability to reach his lines the *poilus* perceived the fact and with yells they leaped to the rescue, scrambling from their trenches in a wild charge against the Huns.

The aeroplane fell into a shell hole some forty yards short of the French lines and was smashed to pieces, but the charmed pilot was thrown free of the wreck and was absolutely without injury when his rescuing comrades picked him up and surrounding him carried him hurriedly to their protecting trenches. He is credited with saying, when they marvelled at his escape, "I was born on Christmas Eve. They cannot hurt me."

M. Bordeaux, who is a loving biographer, devotes over three hundred pages to the events and deeds of the amazing hero, and there is not with it all an event recorded that is not worthy the record. Among them is an instance of the irony of fate that occasionally turns intended service into serious hurt. It was in September, 1916, in the Somme battle. Guynemer had shot down two Boche machines and was after a third at an altitude of 10,000 feet when a foolishly fired French shell meant for the enemy machine caught him in full flight, breaking a wing and taking off part of his radiator.

Of course, the machine began falling to the earth. By energetic efforts with the controls and the swing of his body Guynemer succeeded in checking the fall and establishing a glide, but he could not lessen the velocity with which he was approaching the ground. The catastrophe was witnessed by the troops and when the Spad crashed head first they ran to take up the remains of the doomed pilot. But when they reached the spot there stood Guynemer unharmed regarding mournfully the wreck of his machine. An idea of the force of the impact may be had from the fact that the nose of the machine was driven so deep that it could not be budged.

The jubilant soldiers lifted Guynemer to their shoulders and bore him to the general's quarters. The general embraced him and ordered the troops to form for review. Then the adored aviator was led by the general down the lines. One can imagine the enthusiasm, the emotions of the French.

Won Without Arms

Guynemer kept a diary of all his doings day by day, and his biographer makes free use of it. His method of entry was laconic. He never stressed a point. Take as an example of the style and as a character sketch of the man his entry of January 26, 1917, when he did that incredible thing, brought down and captured a two-seater enemy machine when he himself was without offensive arms. He went up in a borrowed machine of which he was sufficiently contemptuous. The day before he had not gone up. His only diary entry for that day was *"Je regarde voler les autres et ronge."*

The translation of his entry for the 26th is as follows:

> Bucquet lends me his taxi. Gun sights nothing, simply an emptiness. What a layout! Line of aim worse than pitiful.
> 12 o'clock saw a Boche at 12,000 feet. Up went the lift. Arrived in the sun. In tacking about was caught in nasty tail spin. Descending, I see the Boche 400 yards behind, firing at me. Recovering I fire ten shots. Gun jams completely. But the Boche seemed to feel some emotion and dived away full south with his motor wide open. Let's follow him!
> But I do not get too close to him, for fear he will see that I can't shoot. Altimeter drops to 5,000 feet above Estries-Saint-Denis. I manoeuvre my Boche as nicely as I can, and suddenly he redresses and sets off towards Rheims.
> I essay a bluff. I mount to 2,000 feet over him and drop on to him like a stone. Made an impression on him but was begin-

ning to believe it did not take when he suddenly began to descend. I put myself 10 yards behind him; but every time I showed my nose around the edge of his tail the gunner took aim at me.

We take the road towards Compiegne—3,000 feet—2,000 feet again I show my nose, and this time the gunner stands up, takes his hands from his machine gun and motions to me that he surrenders. *All Right!*

I see underneath his machine the four bombs in their resting place. 1,500 feet. The Boche slows down his windmill. 600 feet. 300 feet. I swerve over him while he lands. I make a round or two at 300 feet and see that I am over an airdrome. But not having any gun or cartridges I cannot prevent them from setting fire to their taxi, a 200 H. P. Albatross, magnificent.

When I see they are surrounded I come down and show the two Boches my disabled machine gun. Some headpiece!

They had fired 200 shots at me. My ten bullets that I fired before I jammed had struck their altimeter and the revolution counter, hence their emotion! The pilot told me that my aeroplane I shot down day before yesterday at Goyancourt had gunner killed and pilot wounded in the knee. Hope this unique confirmation will be accepted by authorities. It will make my 30th.

The Flight into the Unknown

But after he had brought down his fiftieth, for some unaccountable reason a change came over Guynemer. He became nervous and irritable. He lost his old vivacity, nerve, dash, and with them his instincts of the air seemed to desert him. Friends urged him to rest, to give over fighting and direct his genius to teaching others to fly. But he answered: "They would say I would fight no more because France has no more decorations to give me"; and he had a jealous pride to work harder than ever, do even more valiant deeds. And he did work harder. He did take greater risks.

He engaged in combats but was unable to win. Luck had turned and his chums, his comrades, knew him to be a sick man in no condition to fly. They 'phoned to their commanding officer in Paris begging him to come and take Guynemer away for a recuperative rest. Captain Brocard responded promptly. He arrived at the Dunkerque aerodrome at nine o'clock the next morning. But Guynemer had ordered his machine and taken flight half an hour before, accompanied, in another machine, by Lieut. Bozon-Verduras.

It was Sept. 11, 1918. It was Guynemer's last flight. All that is known of it Bozon-Verduras tells. Somewhat northeast of Ypres, at an altitude of 12,000 feet, a two-seater enemy machine was discovered. Directing Lieut. Bozon-Verduras to take a position above to guard against rescue, Guynemer rushed to the attack. While on guard the lieutenant detected a distant enemy formation and drove forward to intercept its course. But without seeing him) the formation changed its course and the lieutenant returned to position. He did not, however, see Guynemer's machine, nor did several hours of extended search lead to any trace above or below of the vanished aviator. His fuel exhausted, the lieutenant returned to the aerodrome hoping Guynemer might be there. But he was not. All day they waited for his return. He never returned. "Undoubtedly," said someone of the men, "he has been taken prisoner."

Says M. Bordeaux:

> Guynemer a prisoner! He had said one day, laughingly, 'The Boche will never have me alive'—but his laugh was terrible. No one believed Guynemer to be a prisoner. What then?

Nothing more is known. The Germans made contradictory and unreliable reports about his death. The simple minded among the French believe their hero an immortal, taken up into his native heaven. The lofty minded French name him "*Héros légendaire, tombé en plein ciel de gloire, après trois ans de lutte ardente*," and this they have inscribed on a marble plaque in the crypt of the Pantheon, that temple which the French hold sacred as the "Sepulcher of Great Men."

WORTHY CITATION

A Distinguished Service on the Battle Front for Which No Honours Provision has Been Made

There is a kind of heroism that never gets tagged. Many would not think it heroism. But when you come to analyse heroism into its elemental parts you find that it is a spiritual energy with myriad forms of expression, though these forms always have the character of self-dedication to an altruistic service. By that definition Capt. E. W. Zinn takes place in the ranks of war heroes; but if you have not seen what *The Stars and Stripes*—the official newspaper of the A. E. F., published in France—has said about him you probably never have heard of Capt.

Zinn and his self-appointed mission. It is well to know about him; so here is the story as it appeared in the official organ:

> It was Captain Zinn, a veteran of the French Foreign Legion and the Lafayette Escadrille, who, when eager young American aviators, fresh from their training-camps, reported for duty where the fighting was, assigned them to squadrons and each to a particular airplane. Thus, it was that he came to know them all. He sent them to their stations. He knew what ships they would pilot in combat in the air, on bombing expeditions, on reconnaissances over the lines.
>
> And now he seeks for those he sent out and who never returned. He asked that he might do it. If you talk to Captain Zinn about it, you know why he made the request. You know how he feels about that which he is doing. There is no mawkish sentiment about Captain Zinn.
>
> But deep down within him Captain Zinn feels that he and no other should go out on the mission that now engages him. He has an interest that is intimate and personal.
>
> Already, Captain Zinn's quest has led him over the greater part of northern France and into Belgium and Germany. Through the torn fields and woods in the Verdun, Château-Thierry, St. Mihiel, and Meuse sectors he has gone. He has tramped through the Argonne to Sedan and sought in the mountains that encircle Metz and hide the valley of the Moselle. Wherever there was fighting in which the American Air Service participated, there has gone, or will go, Zinn.
>
> Out of 150 missing American aviators, Captain Zinn already has definitely located and identified the spots where seventy fell and were buried. It has required many days of painstaking search and inquiry to attain this result.
>
> Captain Zinn has found that in a great many cases American fliers were buried either by the Germans or by civilians with no mark of identification left on them.
>
> ### The Unidentified
>
> Many times, he has come upon a grave with a rude cross on which was scrawled: 'Unidentified American Aviator' or 'Two Unidentified American Aviators.' He has had to obtain positive identification by careful examination of air-service records, questioning of peasants and civilians who saw American ma-

ATHLETES AMONG FRENCH AIRMEN
Georges Carpentier, heavyweight boxer (the second figure from the left).

chines brought down and deductions based on the information he gathered. In some instances, it has been necessary to open graves to make sure.

To start out with, Captain Zinn has the records of squadrons, which show, for instance, on what date a missing pilot went out, what his mission was, over what country he naturally would go, and what kind of machine he had. Perhaps an attack by an overwhelming force or an accident or other circumstances forced the pilot off the course marked out for him. When he failed to return, only speculation as to where he fell could be indulged in. Unless the Germans notified his squadron of his death and the location of his grave, he became one of the men for whom Captain Zinn now seeks.

There was the case of young Kenyon Roper, of the 91st Aero Squadron. By a process of elimination of facts gathered, it was fairly definitely established that Roper had come down in the night between the lines. Captain Zinn questions scores of peasant folk. But the search appeared to be hopeless. And then Captain Zinn heard that a small boy had a handkerchief that the dead flier had possessed. He found the boy and the handkerchief. And written in indelible ink on the little piece of linen was the name '*Kenyon Roper.*' It was easy then to learn from the boy where the grave was and to be sure that Kenyon Roper lay sleeping there. (*The 90th & 91st Aero Squadrons, Two Accounts of American Pilots and Aircraft During the First World War* by Leland M. Carver Gustaf A. Lindstrom A. T. Foster George C. Kenney Horace Moss Guilbert is published by Leonaur).

A Last Autograph

Then there was the case of Lester Harter, of the 11th Squadron. He went out and his machine caught fire. Harter jumped, just as Major Lufbery did and as other aviators have done, and fell many thousand feet to his death. When awe-stricken peasants ran from the fields to his crushed body they found in his hand a scrap of paper, and on it was written in hurried, jerky letters, '*Lester Harter.*'

Fearing lost identity among the dead, Lester Harter must have written his name on that piece of paper before he jumped from his machine.

Then there were Kinne and McElroy, of the 99th Aero Squadron. Only a piece of the tail of their machine was found. Their plane came down in flames between Cunel and Nantillois. Both jumped. One day their squadron commander joined in the search for their bodies. He hunted for hours in a thick wood. And he gave up. He was standing on the edge of a covered shell-hole, discouraged. Some impulse caused him to stir the earth in the shell-hole with his foot. And there he found the body of young McElroy. Nearby they later found Kinne.

There are many such stories that Captain Zinn can tell.

From the information he gathers, Captain Zinn writes personal letters to the relatives of the dead aviators, telling in simple words how and where they went to their deaths. His letters usually give the first true account of the manner in which the fighters of the air met their ends. Sometimes those letters destroy cherished hopes that the aviators reported as 'missing' by the War Department might some time, somehow, turn up. But it is better so, says Captain Zinn.

A Challenge Duel

The Guns of Both Armies Suspend Fire as Captains Ball and Immelman Fight in Air

It was often said in the early months of the war that the air combats revived the spirit of ancient chivalry. It was true for a time, but German treachery and ruthlessness soon changed the character of the upper warfare. When the raider and the dastard entered, gallantry necessarily gave way to grim and merciless antagonism.

There were many, though, on both sides who felt that no glory came to aviation from methods of frightfulness and reprisals for such frightfulness and to the last there were instances of clean, brave fights. One of the last duels on the knightly lines of conduct was that in which Captain Immelman, "The Falcon" of the German Army, met Captain Ball, one of the most brilliant airmen of the British Royal Flying Corps. Immelman had a record, of some fifty-one British airplanes downed. Captain Ball wanted to wipe out this record, and the daring German at the same time; so, one day he flew over the German lines and dropped the following note:

Captain Immelman:
I challenge you to a man-to-man fight to take place this afternoon at two o'clock. I will meet you over the German lines.

Have your anti-aircraft guns withhold their fire, while we decide which is the better man. The British guns will be silent.

Ball.

Ball was by that time quite renowned. The Germans were aware of his official record. He had taken part in twenty-six combats, had destroyed eleven hostile machines, driven two out of control, and forced several others to land.

In these combats Captain Ball had gone up alone. On one occasion, he had fought six hostile machines, twice he had fought five machines, and once four. When leading two other British aeroplanes he had attacked an enemy formation of eight. On each of these occasions he had brought down at least one enemy.

The Germans knew all that, but evidently Ball had picked an opponent worthy of him not only in skill but in courage and chivalry, for that day the answer to the note was dropped from a German machine:

Captain Ball:
Your challenge is accepted. The guns will not interfere. I will meet you promptly at two.

Immelmann.

CHEERS FROM OPPOSING TRENCHES

Far and wide along the trenches the word was spread. Firing stopped as though a flag of truce had been hoisted. Germans and English left covers and sought positions of vantage from which to watch the battle royal. At the appointed time both flyers rose promptly and made their way over "No Man's Land."

An eyewitness relates:

Cheering arose. There were wild cheers for Ball. The Germans yelled just as vigorously for Immelman.
The cheers from the trenches continued; the Germans' increased in volume; ours changed into cries of alarm.

Immelman was known to have a method of attack peculiar to himself. Instead of approaching his adversary from the side, he manoeuvred to get squarely behind him. His study was to hold the nose of his machine almost on the tail of the aircraft he was pursuing. This gave him, Abbot points out, what used to be called in the Navy a raking position, for his shots would rake the whole body of the enemy airplane from tail to nose with a fair chance of hitting either the fuel tank, the engine, or the pilot. Failing to secure the position he coveted, this daring German would surrender it with apparent unconcern to the enemy, who usually fell into a trap. For just as the foeman's machine came up to the tail of Immelman's craft the latter would suddenly turn his nose straight to earth, drop like a stone, execute a backward loop and come up behind his surprised adversary, who thus found the tables suddenly turned...

We have left the description of the duel with the English in alarm. The eyewitness continues:

> Ball, thousands of feet above us and only a speck in the sky, was doing the craziest things imaginable. He was below Immelman and was apparently making no effort to get above him and thus gaining the advantage of position. Rather he was swinging around, this way and that, attempting, it seemed, to postpone the inevitable.
>
> We saw the German's machine dip over preparatory to starting the nose dive.
>
> 'He's gone now,' sobbed a young soldier at my side, for he knew Immelman's gun would start its raking fire once it was being driven straight down.
>
> Then in a fraction of a second the tables were turned. Before Immelman's plane could get into firing position, Ball drove his machine into a loop, getting above his adversary and cutting loose with his gun and smashing Immelman by a hail of bullets as he swept by.

A Wreath for His Victim

> Immelman's airplane burst into flames and dropped. Ball from above followed for a few hundred feet and then straightened out and raced for home. He settled down, rose again, hurried back, and released a huge wreath of flowers, almost directly over the spot where Immelman's charred body was being lifted from a tangled mass of metal.

Four days later Ball too was killed.

Shortly before his death Ball wrote to a friend:

> You will be pleased to hear that I have ten more Huns, and that my total is now 40—two in front of my French rival. Oh, I'm having a topping time! Today or tomorrow I'm being presented to Sir Douglas Haig. Am very pleased. I just want to get a few

1st Lieut. Philip Benson

Volunteered for night bombing and was particularly efficient in "*chassi*" work. He gave the Germans a taste of their own medicine—by dropping bombs on German towns and firing upon German supply trains.

more if I can.

Ball's wish was gratified. He got more than a few more and then—died as he had so often lived—fighting against great odds, for when last seen, on the evening of May 7, 1917, he was high above the enemy's lines engaging three German machines at once.

What slender hope had been left for him was shattered by the War Office intimation that Ball had been killed. The brave young officer lost his life at a village 5½ miles east of La Bassée.

An American Wonder

The Brief but Greatly Achieving Career of Lieut. Frank Luke, Jr.—His Mysterious End

Innumerable are the instances, never to be reckoned, of the sudden meteoric flame of splendid daring—the sudden flash of the courageous soul in achievement, and the equally sudden extinction—that a thousand attested circumstances assure us characterized the terrible passing of the Great War. Happily, for the world, always the better for new evidence that "divinity still lives in the hearts of men," very many of those deeds of devoted heroism have been written into history for the inspiration of high-minded youth.

There was no experience more aptly described as meteoric than that of Frank Luke, Jr., who joined the 27th Aero Squadron near Château-Thierry late in July, 1918, did brilliant service in that connection, and before the end of September had utterly disappeared from the knowledge of men—one of the missing never definitely accounted for.

Frank was a Phoenix, Arizona, boy, barely twenty when he entered the service. After a period of training in Texas he was sent to France and had further training at Isoudun and was then sent to join the squadron near Château-Thierry. He was an enthusiast for flying, never getting enough of it.

It was like second nature to him, and he adhered to no rules but his own, apparently indifferent to safety regulations when in the air, and so impatient of restrictions that he almost invariably got lost from his flight when it went out in formation. This gave rise among his fellows to the belief that he was afraid to follow, his getting lost being the deliberate result of "funk." In course of time, however, they came to understand that Frank Luke held no acquaintance with fear. He simply had a method—method and initiative—and put his abilities to

LIEUTENANT FRANK LUKE
He joined an Aero Squadron near Château-Thierry, late in July, 1918, and before the end of September he disappeared without being heard from again.

their most effective use. It was so good a method, so wisely reasoned and so admirably executed that in the space of seventeen days he shot down eighteen enemy balloons and planes.

Lieut. Col. Harold E. Hartney, Chief of Gunnery in the Air Service, at that time Commander of the Squadron to which Luke belonged, gave an account of the young aviator's first exploit. August 6, 1918, the First Pursuit Group, which included the 27th Squadron, was operating on the Château-Thierry sector. The work was seriously interfered with by heavy barrages of pursuit planes maintained by the enemy to prevent Allied reconnaissance over the territory being evacuated. Col. Hartney says:

His First Exploit

Lieut. Luke believed that if he could get across the opposing lines unobserved and far enough, he would be able to take the enemy formations unaware and swoop down upon the unsuspecting rear man, shoot him down and get away in safety. Accordingly, one day he went off on his own at great altitude and crossed over into enemy territory. Far below him he spied an enemy formation of six machines dropping down to land on their own aerodrome. Perfectly aware of the odds against him, he swooped from 15,000 feet to 3,000 feet in one long dive, speeding at approximately 200 miles an hour, closed in on the rear man, and from a distance of no more than twenty yards sent him crashing down.

The enemy formation had been taken completely by surprise. Before they could realize what had happened or engage Luke in combat the latter dropped to an elevation of less than 400 feet, and, zigzagging, made his way home, dodging anti-aircraft fire and machinegun nests until he crossed the lines. By then he was completely out of gasoline and was compelled to make a forced landing near the front line. He had seen the enemy machine crash to earth, but was unable to give the location, and therefore he could not get from eye-witnesses on the ground the confirmation required to make the victory official.

That feat indicated the man. It was very soon apparent that on the occasions when he was "lost" he was off on adventures of his own, planning actions and studying the means to execute them,—qualifying himself for what he conceived to be his most valuable and effective service. He was a veritable hunter.

The morning set for the opening of the St. Mihiel offensive, Sept. 12, 1918, the clouds hung low and the weather was such that ordinarily it would have been regarded as altogether unfit for flying. But Luke was not to be deterred by it. He was off at dawn in quest of enemy planes or balloons and after many vain explorations he finally discovered a German balloon at the extreme right of the American sector, but operated against a portion of the line allotted to other flyers.

He returned to his aerodrome, and on reporting the balloon learned that it had been doing great damage by an enfilading fire, but that it had been attacked repeatedly without success both by American and French aviators. Luke offered to destroy the balloon and set off with Lieut. Fritz Wehner, his flying partner. The statement of eye-witnesses from the ground was that Luke dived suddenly out of the clouds taking the balloon wholly by surprise, but the balloon-gun which he was handling for the first time jammed when he attempted to discharge it. He rose into the clouds, got the gun free, immediately dived again and fired the heavy incendiary bullet that sent the balloon down in flames.

Downed Three Balloons in One Day

Two days later he sent another balloon flaming down in somewhat more exciting circumstances. While he was speeding with an escort of other pilots, to attack three enemy balloons operating at an unusually low altitude, his escort became engaged with a formation of Fokkers. This would have made it seem to many pilots unwise to proceed with the attack; but Luke took advantage of the fight above to dive down and begin the assault on one of the balloons which, after several attempts, he succeeded in shooting down, though machine bullets and anti-aircraft shells and flaming onions were showered about him. As the balloon fell burning, Luke flew down to close range and turned loose his machine gun on the Huns on the ground with the desired result of many casualties.

When he got back home he found that his machine was so full of bullet-holes that a very few more taps would have weakened it enough to bring it down in collapse. But within five minutes he was in another machine and begging leave to go on a further quest.

At 5 o'clock that afternoon he sent down the second balloon in flames. Later he discovered attempts being made to send up another balloon north of Verdun; he hastened back to his squadron and asked to be ordered out at dusk to surprise and destroy the big bag.

He left with instructions not to descend on the balloon until 7.50

(that being for the benefit of his protective escort who would follow him down a few moments later). Precisely at 7.50 the watchers on the aerodrome saw the balloon flare in the darkness and fall to the ground.

And so, the story runs; each new adventure a companion thriller to the others, every machine in which he flew being more or less riddled with bullets, and the miracle is that the daring youth passed so many hazards unscathed. Col. Hartney is authority for the statement that balloon strafing is in reality "the most dangerous exploit any man in any branch of the service can undertake."

Frank Luke in seventeen days accounted for eighteen enemy balloons and planes. He was the first American flyer to win the Congressional Medal of Honour.

His End a Mystery

But there is an end to successful adventures as to other things, and the brilliant career of this Arizona lad came to abrupt conclusion, leaving the shadow of mystery as to just how the hero passed on. Here is the story of the last exploit as Col. Hartley tells it:

> His next official victory was on Sept. 28, when he shot down a German *Hanoveraner* airplane which was being escorted by a single-seater *Fokker*.
>
> That evening he did not return to his own aerodrome, but remained all night with the French squadron and went out the next day for the express purpose of destroying three balloons. The wonderful story of his exciting fight against hopeless odds and of his glorious death need not be dwelt upon. For his work on Sept. 29 he was awarded the Medal of Honour.
>
> Briefly, what happened was that he flew over an American aerodrome and dropped a weighted message. The message asked that a lookout be kept for three *drachens* over on the German side. He was next seen to go over in that direction at a very high altitude, and when very nearly over the *drachens* was attacked by ten enemy machines. He engaged all of them single-handed and crashed two of the ten. Then he dropped—out of control, as it seemed, but most likely only pretending to be so. When he reached the level of the balloons he shot them down one after another in flames—all three of them. The anti-aircraft guns were very busy about the second balloon. After that he disappeared.

Beyond this all that is known is more or less speculative. Jan. 3, 1919, the Graves Registration officer of Neufchateau reported to the Chief of the A. E. F. Air Service on the subject of the grave of an unknown American aviator, killed Sept. 29, 1918, in the village of Murvaux (Meuse), and asked for possible information to identify the body.

> Reported as having light hair, young, of medium height and rugged physique. Reported by the inhabitants that previous to being killed this man brought down three German balloons, two German planes and dropped hand bombs, killed eleven German soldiers and wounded a number of others. He was wounded himself in the shoulder and evidently had to make a forced landing, and upon landing opened fire with his automatic and fought until he was killed. It is also reported that the Germans took his shoes, leggings and money, leaving his grave unmarked.

Supporting the report is an affidavit (Jan. 15, 1919) signed by twelve inhabitants of the village that gives the foregoing facts in detail and adds this:

> Certify equally to have seen the German *commandant* of the village refuse to have straw placed on the cart carrying the dead aviator to the village cemetery. This same officer drove away some women bringing a sheet to serve as a shroud for the hero, and said, kicking the body, 'Get that out of my way as quick as possible.'

Two of the villagers placed the body on the cart.

ONE TO TWENTY-TWO

The Formidable Odds Against Which a Young English Pilot Daringly Battled, Only to Fall 14,000 Feet into the Sea

German air-raids on London which were entirely without military justification, being a part of the scheme of frightfulness, resulted in the death of relatively few persons; but they roused British resentment to a pitch that had a tremendous influence upon the fighting spirit of the soldiers at the front and the aviators summoned to the defence of London.

In one of the later raids, Lieutenant I. E. R. Young, of the Royal Flying Corps, lost his life in highly dramatic circumstances that proved his heroic quality. The event is best recorded, perhaps, in a letter written by Young's commanding officer to the father of the daring aviator. The letter was as follows:

> Your son, as you know, had only been in my squadron for a short time, but quite long enough for me to realise what a very efficient and gallant officer he was. He had absolutely the heart of a lion and was a very good pilot. Your son had been up on every raid of late, and had always managed to get in contact with the enemy machines. The last raid, which unfortunately resulted in his death, shows what a very gallant officer we have lost.
> Almost single-handed he flew straight into the middle of the twenty-two machines, and both himself and his observer at once opened fire. All the enemy machines opened fire also, so he was horribly outnumbered. The volume of fire to which he was subjected was too awful for words. To give you a rough idea: There were twenty-two machines, each machine had four guns, and each gun was firing about 400 rounds per minute. Your son never hesitated in the slightest. He flew straight on until, as I should imagine, he must have been riddled with bullets. The machine then put its nose right up in the air and fell over, and went spinning down into the sea from 14,000 feet.
> I, unfortunately, had to witness the whole ghastly affair. The machine sank so quickly that it was, I regret, impossible to save your son's body, he was so badly entangled in the wires, etc. H. M. S. ——— rushed to the spot as soon as possible, but only arrived in time to pick up your son's observer, who, I regret to state, is also dead. He was wounded six times, and had a double fracture in the skull.

FROM SADDLE TO COCKPIT

It Was a Problem of Mud That Turned Trooper Bishop Into an "Ace" of the Royal Flying Corps

It was not unnatural that intrepidity in the air should have commanded more of public attention and enthusiasm during the war than did the courage, daring and amazing fortitude of the men in the trenches. The sensation of novelty makes stronger appeal to the curious interest of humanity than do deeds and events no less masterful though more familiar to experience. So it was that the invaders of the air, who fought their duels or delivered their assaults above the clouds,

Colonel William A. Bishop,
a Canadian "Ace" of the Royal Flying Corps

came in for the lion's share of the popular plaudits,—the miracles of the flyers having the advantage of the romantic and picturesque over the miracles of the men who kept their feet on the earth. That is why there are more stories of the one than of the other. But are they not wonder stories? The career of any of the "Aces," American, French, British, Italian, German, compels an affirmative answer.

Among the many is that of Col. William A. Bishop, a Canadian member of the British Royal Flying Corps, his story rather the more interesting by reason of his living to tell it himself after the battles of the air had ceased. He had a record of forty-nine German planes and balloons actually destroyed. In addition to this, he was the victor in eighty to a hundred other fights high in air, the enemy engaged being driven from the field, either because of wounds or of that discretion said to be the better part of valour. In recognition of these achievements he received the Victoria Cross, the Distinguished Service Order, twice bestowed, and the Military Cross—all in a single fighting season and before he was twenty-three years of age.

Perhaps the most remarkable thing about it all was that the hero of these officially honoured achievements was little known, until the war ended, to the public at large. But that was due to the fact that the British policy was not to emphasize the performances of one branch of the service more than those of another. It is claimed that there were about forty "aces" of the British Royal Flying Corps of whom the world has never heard. Only when there was repeated mention of a name in The Official Gazette was the public made aware that a flyer had won exceptional title to honours.

Bishop went to England as a cavalry officer in a unit of the Second Canadian Division, and expected that his services would be in the saddle, not in the cockpit. That was in July, 1915, in a period of torrential rains and consequent mud—cheer-despoilers of a cavalry camp. It was while wallowing in knee-deep mud that he viewed with envy a pilot gliding overhead in a trim little aeroplane, and the sudden desire possessed him to follow that airy mind-free branch of the service. He talked with a friend in the Royal Flying Corps who approved his purpose, and assured him the transfer could be made quite easily. He got the transfer and was soon training as an observer, his first lessons being flights in a ponderous training "bus" (as the airmen name their planes) that was not equal to a speed of more than fifty miles an hour. In a few months, he got the observer's badge or insignia, an O with a spread wing attached to one side, and within a little while was making observations and taking photographs in France over the enemy lines.

This useful work, so highly important to the men fighting on the ground, was drudgery to him because he was burning to become a fighter. Some six months later his longing was gratified; he returned to England and set about acquiring the knowledge and skill to fly "on his own." He had the usual experience of the beginner,—elation over his first "solo"; uncertainties, anxieties as to how to get back to earth safely; a somewhat humiliating landing, etc.; but he suffered no misadventure. The first week in March, 1917, he landed in Boulogne with ten or twelve other flying men for his second experience on the fighting front.

Keeping Up with the Formation

The first time he was to go over the lines his orders were to bring up the rear of a flight of six machines, and he found keeping up with the formation such a busying task that he could be conscious of little else. He says:

> Every time the formation turned or did anything unexpected, it took me two or three minutes to get back in my proper place. But I got back every time as fast as I could. I felt safe when I was with the formation and scared when I was out of it, for I had been warned many times that it is a fatal mistake to get detached and become a straggler. And I had heard of German 'head hunters' too. They are German machines that fly very high and avoid combat with anything like an equal number, but are quick to pounce down upon a straggler, or an Allied machine that has been damaged and is bravely struggling to get home. Fine sportsmanship that!
>
> The way I clung to my companions that day reminded me of the little child hanging to its mother's skirts while crossing a street. I remember I also felt as a child does when it is going up a dark pair of stairs and is sure something is going to reach out somewhere and grab it. I was so intent on the clinging part that I paid very little attention to anything else.

Some distance off was another formation on patrol that became engaged with a Hun formation and he saw the young flyer of one of the machines, "one of our own," going down in flames, but his reflections on that incident were suddenly interrupted by a "*bang*" of terrifying violence close to his ears. The tail of his machine shot

IN FORMATION

These airplanes have ascended early in the morning for battle formation. The range of vision is interesting from this altitude.

up in the air and he fell three or more hundred feet before he could recover control. It was a shot from an "Archie" (an anti-aircraft gun), and Colonel Bishop says of it:

> That shot, strange to relate, was the closest I have ever had from anti-aircraft fire.

The German "Flying Pig"

In his highly entertaining book, *Winged Warfare*, (also published by Leonaur), Colonel Bishop introduces an amusing incident as the finish of this night's patrol. He says:

> We continued to patrol our beat, and I was keeping my place so well I began to look about a bit. After one of these gazing spells, I was startled to discover that the three leading machines of our formation were missing. Apparently, they had disappeared into nothingness. I looked around hastily, and then discovered them underneath me, diving rapidly. I didn't know just what they were diving at, but I dived, too.
>
> Long before I got down to them, however, they had been in a short engagement half a mile below me, and had succeeded in frightening off an enemy artillery machine which had been doing wireless observation work. It was a large white German two-seater, and I learned after we landed that it was a well-known machine and was commonly called 'the flying pig.' Our patrol leader had to put up with a lot of teasing that night because he had attacked the 'pig.' It seems that it worked every day on this part of the front, was very old, had a very bad pilot and a very poor observer to protect him.
>
> It was a sort of point of honour in the squadron that the decrepit old 'pig' should not actually be shot down. It was considered fair sport, however, to frighten it. Whenever our machines approached, the 'pig' would begin a series of clumsy turns and ludicrous manoeuvres, and would open a frightened fire from ridiculously long ranges. The observer was a very bad shot and never succeeded in hitting any of our machines, so attacking this particular German was always regarded more as a joke than a serious part of warfare.
>
> The idea was only to frighten the 'pig,' but our patrol leader had made such a determined dash at him the first day we went over that he never appeared again. For months, the patrol leader was

chided for playing such a nasty trick upon a harmless old Hun.

As Colonel Bishop's story is that of one thrilling and perilous adventure following fast upon another, it is impossible to give his career in detail or recount even the chief of his many engagements. The fight in which he won the Military Cross is a good illustration of the clear judgment and fearlessness which characterized his exploits in general.

The Allies had been preparing for the great offensive that began with the battle of Arras, and for a week in advance of the date set for the initiative (April 9th, 1917) the airmen had been carrying out orders to keep the sky free from prying eyes of men in planes and to attack and destroy enemy observation balloons. The balloons flew from the same places every day because there were batteries of antiaircraft guns stationed below that area.

Bishop was assigned to the destruction of a particularly annoying balloon that went up daily in contempt of scouting planes. The balloon, because of cloudy weather, did not go up the first day after the assignment. The character of the fighting may be determined from the fact that in two days, April 6 and 7, the Allies lost twenty-eight machines as against fifteen German machines accounted for. But, says Bishop:

> We considered this a small price to pay for the amount of work accomplished and the number of machines engaged (every class of machine was thrown into the clearing process) coupled with the fact that all our work was done within the German lines.

How He Won the Military Cross

My own experiences on the seventh of April brought me my first decoration—the Military Cross. The thrills were all condensed into a period of two minutes for me. In that time, I was fortunate enough to shoot down an enemy machine and destroy the 'sausage' I had started for two days before. This should have been excitement enough, but I added to it by coming within fifteen feet of being taken a German prisoner and becoming an unwilling guest of the Huns for the 'duration.'

I was ordered after my particular balloon and had climbed to about 5,000 feet before heading for the lines. On my way, there I had to pass over one of our own observation balloons. I don't know what it was that attracted my attention, but looking down I saw what appeared to be two men descending in parachutes.

A moment later the balloon below me burst into flames. I saw the enemy machine which had set it on fire engaged with some of ours, but as I had definite orders to proceed straight to the lines and destroy the hostile balloon which had been allotted to me, I was unable to join in the fighting.

Just about this time an amusing incident was in progress at our aerodrome. A colonel of the corps was telephoning my squadron commander, informing him that one of our balloons had just been destroyed.

'Well, if it is any consolation, young Bishop, of my squadron, has just gone over to get one of theirs,' replied my commander. 'Good God,' said the colonel, 'I hope he has not made a mistake in the balloon and set ours on fire.'

At this moment, I was serenely sailing over the enemy trenches keeping a sharp lookout

At this moment, I was serenely sailing over the enemy trenches keeping a sharp lookout for some sign of my own balloon. After flying five miles over the lines I discovered it and circled around as a preliminary to diving down upon it. But just then I heard the rattle of machine guns directly behind me and saw bullet holes appear as if by magic in the wings of my machine. I pulled back as if to loop, sending the nose of my machine straight up into the air.

As I did so the enemy scout shot by underneath me. I stood on my tail for a moment or two, then let the machine drop back, put her nose down and dived after the Hun, opening fire straight behind him at very close range. He continued to dive away with increasing speed and later was reported to have crashed just under where the combat had taken place. This victory I put down entirely to luck. The man flew directly in line with my gun and it would have been impossible to have missed him.

I proceeded now to dive for the balloon, but having had so much warning, it had been pulled down to the ground. I would have been justified in going home when I saw this, for our orders were not to go under 1,000 feet after the sausages. But I was just a bit peevish with this particular balloon, and to a certain extent my blood was up. So, I decided to attack the ungainly monster in its 'bed.' I dived straight for it and when about 500 feet from the ground, opened fire. Nothing happened. So, I

COLONEL BISHOP INSPECTING A LEWIS AIRCRAFT GUN

continued to dive and fire rapid bursts until I was only fifty feet above the bag. Still there were no signs of it catching fire. I then turned my machine gun on the balloon crew who were working frantically on the ground. They scattered and ran all about the field. Meantime a 'flaming onion' battery was attempting to pelt me with those unsavoury missiles, so I whirled upon them with a burst of twenty rounds or more. One of the onions had flared within a hundred yards of me.

Suddenly My Engine Had Failed

This was all very exciting, but suddenly, with a feeling of faintness, I realised that my engine had failed. I thought that again, as during my first fight, the engine had oiled up from the steep diving I had done. It seemed but a moment before that I was coming down at a speed that must have been nearly 200 miles an hour. But I had lost it all in turning my machine upon the people on the ground.

There was no doubt in my mind this time as to just where I was, and there appeared no alternative but to land and give myself up. Underneath me was a large open field with a single tree in it. I glided down, intending to strike the tree with one wing just at the moment of landing, thus damaging the machine so it would be of little use to the Huns, without injuring myself.

A Miraculous Recovery

I was within fifteen feet of the ground, absolutely sick at heart with the uselessness of it all, my thoughts having turned to home and the worry they would all feel when I was reported in the list of the missing, when without warning one of my nine cylinders gave a kick. Then a second one miraculously came to life, and in another moment the old engine—the best old engine in all the world—had picked up with a roar on all the nine cylinders. Once again, the whole world changed for me. In less time than it takes to tell it I was tearing away for home at a hundred miles an hour.

My greatest safety from attack now lay in keeping close to the ground, and this I did. The 'Archies' cannot fire when you are so close to earth, and few pilots would have risked a dive at me at the altitude which I maintained. The machine guns on the ground rattled rather spitefully several times, but worried me not at all. I had had my narrow squeak for this day and nothing could stop me now.

I even had time to glance back over my shoulder, and there, to my great joy, I saw a cloud of smoke and flames rising from my erstwhile *bête noir*—the sausage. We afterward learned it was completely destroyed.

It was a strange thing to be skimming along just above the ground in enemy territory. From time to time I would come on groups of Huns who would attempt to fire on me with rifles and pistols, but I would dart at them and they would immediately scatter and run for cover. I flew so low that when I would come to a clump of trees I would have to pull my nose straight up toward the sky and 'zoom' over them. Most of the Germans were so startled to see me right in their midst, as it were, they either forgot to fire or fired so badly as to insure my absolute safety. Crossing the three lines of German trenches was not so comfortable, but by zigzagging and quick dodging I negotiated them safely and climbed away to our aerodrome. There I found that no bullets had passed very close to me, although my wingtips were fairly perforated.

That evening I was delighted to get congratulations not only from my colonel, but my brigadier as well, supplemented later by a wire from the general commanding the Flying Corps. This I proudly sent home the same evening in a letter.

Like Shooting Clay Pigeons

There seems to be a general feeling among airmen that theirs is not a business or profession, but a game. Colonel Bishop declares that it did not seem to him to be killing a man to bring down a machine:

> It was more as if I were destroying a mechanical target, with no human being in it. Once or twice the idea that a live man had been piloting the machine would occur to me, and it would worry me a bit. My sleep would be spoiled perhaps for a night. I did not relish the idea of killing even Germans, yet, when in a combat in the air, it seemed more like any other kind of sport, and to shoot down a machine was very much the same as if one were shooting down clay pigeons. One has the great satisfaction of feeling that he had hit the target and brought it down; that one was victorious again.

The fascination that such a game has for the airman is easily understood.

Bishop brought down his fortieth enemy plane six miles within the enemy lines, and escaped in spite of a hail of shells from antiaircraft guns for five miles of the return trip, his machine being fairly well riddled; and, one day just at that time, his cup of happiness filled and overflowed with the award of the Victoria Cross.

Dodging "Jack Death"

A German Aviator's Perils and Escapes on an Observation Tour

In the early days of the war, the value of the flying machine as a weapon was not by any means appreciated. It was used for observation and bomb-dropping purposes almost exclusively. The Germans were the first to realize its possibilities as a gunning as well as bombing or spying craft. They began carrying rifles and pistols with which to pot enemy aviators, and the chivalry of the air, so excellent a feature of the initial period, disappeared, for, necessarily the Allied aviators were not slow to follow the lead. It was, however, in the early stage, September, 1914, that the duel occurred of which the following is an account. The narrative was written by the German aviator, the chief figure in the adventure.

The story, the truth of which is unquestioned, was published originally in the Berlin *Tageblatt* from which the *New York Evening Post* made the translation. It is of special interest as a report of one of the first, if not the first of the armed encounters between belligerent planes.

Observing the Retreat of the British

God be thanked! After a veritable Odyssey, I am at last joined again this noon to my division. To be sure, my wanderings were not much to be wondered at, for, during my absence, my troop had advanced about sixty-five kilometres in a south-westerly direction. All the more joyfully, however, was I greeted on all sides, for I had already been given up after an absence of more than four days; and, indeed, I myself wondered, as I made my report to my commander, that Jack Death had so allowed me to slip through his fingers.

On the morning of the 6th of September, I had ascended from D—— with the commission to report the positions of the enemy at S—— and F—— and to make charts of the opposing forces which I observed. First Lieut. K—— went with me as a guest on the flight, and my brave biplane soon bore us at an altitude of about 800 meters above the hostile positions, which were repeatedly sketched and photographed from aloft. As we had expected, we were soon the objective of a lively bombardment, and several times I felt a trembling of the machine, already well known to me, a sign that a shot had struck one of the wings. After a three hours' flight we were able to give our report at the office of the General Staff of the —— Army at M——, and earned for it the warmest praise and half of a broiled chicken and an excellent Havana.

As I was making my "Kiste" ready for flight again in the afternoon, with the help of several drivers of the General Staff auto—that is to say, refilling the benzine tank and carefully patching with linen the places where shots had pierced—I counted four of them, one in the body and three in the wings—a Bavarian officer of the General Staff informed me that he would be glad to observe the retreat of the English along the great military road toward M——. I prepared the machine at once, and ascended at about four o'clock in the afternoon with Major G——, the aforementioned General Staff officer.

Following the road, it was at once obvious that the retreat of the English was a disorderly one, absolutely without plan, that it had apparently occurred to the troops to reach the fortified positions at Paris as soon as possible, and there to make their stand.

At Paris! My flying companion shouted something into my face. Although the noise of the motor drowned it out, I believed that I nevertheless understood what he meant. I glanced at the benzine indicator. I had sufficient fuel. Then I held a direct course to the south, and after a period of about half an hour we saw ahead of us in the grey distance, far, far below, the grey, immeasurable sea of stone that was the chief city of France. At a speed of a hundred kilometres an hour we rushed toward it. It became clearer and plainer. The chain of forts, St. Denis, Montmartre, stood out; from the haze, there raised itself the filigree framework of the Eiffel tower. And now—now we hover over the mellow panorama of Paris.

The "Conqueror" at Paris

There lay the white church of Sacré Coeur, there the Gare du Nord, from which the French thought to leave for across the Rhine; there Notre Dame, there the old "Boul Mich," the Boulevard St. Michel, in the Latin Quarter, where I Bohemianised so long as an art student, and over which I now flew as a conqueror. Unprotected beneath me lay the heart of the enemy, the proud glittering Babel of the Seine. The thought of everything hateful, always attached to the great city, was swallowed up; an emotion of possession, of power, alone remained. And doubly joyful we felt ourselves. Doubly conquerors! In a great circle, I swept over the sea of houses. In the streets raised itself a murmuring of the people, whom the bold "German bird" astonished, who cannot understand how the Germans are turning the French discovery to their own service more cleverly and advantageously than the French themselves.

The Return from Paris

For nearly an hour we had been flying in swoops and had been shot at vainly from here and there below us, when there approached in extremely rapid flight from the direction of Juvisy a French monoplane. Since it was much faster than my biplane, I must turn and seek to escape, while the major made ready my rifle and reached for his revolver. The monoplane came steadily closer and closer; I sought to reach an altitude of 2,000 meters, in order to reach the protecting clouds, but my pursuer, on whom we constantly kept an eye, climbed more rapidly than we. And came always closer and closer. And suddenly I saw at a distance of only about 500 meters still a second biplane, attempting to block my way.

Now it was time to act. In an instant, my companion had grasped the situation. I darted at the flyer before us; then a turn—the major raised the rifle to his cheek. Once, twice, thrice, he fired. Then the hostile machine, now beside us, and hardly a hundred meters away, quivered and then fell like a stone. Our other pursuer had in the meantime reached a position almost over us, and was shooting at us with revolvers. One bullet struck in the body close beside the fuel controller. Then, however, impenetrable mist enfolded us protectingly; and the clouds separated us from the enemy, the sound of whose motor grew ever more distant.

When we came out again from the sea of clouds, it was toward seven o'clock. In order to get our position, we descended, but suddenly there began to burst before us and behind us and beside us roaring shrapnel shells. I found myself still always over hostile positions and exposed to French artillery. "The devil to pay again!" Ever madder grew the fire! I noticed that the machine received blow after blow, but held cold-bloodedly to my course; at the time, it did not come into my mind at all that these little pointed pieces of steel meant death and destruction. Something in mankind remains untouched by knowledge and logic!

There—suddenly before me, a yellow-white burst of flame! The machine bounds upward; at the same time the major shrinks together, blood runs from his shoulder, the wiring of one of the wings is shattered. To be sure, the motor still booms and thunders as before, but the propeller fails. An exploding grenade had knocked it to pieces, torn one of the wings to shreds, and smashed the major's shoulder. Steeply my machine sinks to the ground. By calling up all my power, I succeed in getting the machine into a gliding flight, and I throw the biplane down into the tops of the forest trees. I crash through the branches and tree crowns. I strike heavily, and know no more what goes on around me.

When I wake again from my unconsciousness, I find Major G. lying beside me on the ground, in the midst of a group of Landwehr men. German outposts had recognised me as a friend, and had forced their way into the woods, although only in small numbers, to protect me. Major G. had suffered a severe injury to his shoulder, which made it necessary to transfer him ta the nearest field hospital. I, however, had only sustained a bruise on my leg, and after the application of an emergency bandage remained with the outpost, later to find my way, by all possible—and some impossible—means of transportation, back to my troop.

Warneford's Triumph

The Brilliant Exploit That Marked the First "Down" of a "Zepp" by Airplane

The air raids on the coast towns of England were regarded as the most brutally wanton of the cowardly "frightfulness" tactics of the Germans employed against England. The killing of non-combatants, chiefly women and children, and the destruction of private property were the only material results of those raids, but the moral indignation of the world was aroused. After a period of suspension of this sort of warfare the Germans once more, in June, 1915, began raiding the East and Northeast Coast, the most serious of any that had happened being the raid of June 6.

The raiders sailed over a town on the East Coast during the night and bombed it at their leisure. One large drapery house was struck and was completely wrecked, the entire building—a somewhat old one— collapsing. Adjoining these premises, with only a narrow roadway between, there was one of the most beautiful Norman churches in England. The church was wholly uninjured save a few of the panes in the glass windows. A rumour was spread over the country, and was generally believed, that a large number of girls and women "lived in" on the draper's premises, and were killed when the house was struck.

This rumour was false. The drapery firm had ceased to house its attendants on the premises for a couple of years before the raid. Some working-class streets were very badly damaged, a number of houses destroyed, and many people injured. It was one of the peculiarities of this raid that, unlike results from most of the others, all the people injured were struck while indoors. The total casualties here were twenty-four killed, about sixty seriously injured, and a larger number slightly injured.

The outrage was quickly avenged by a young British naval airman, Flight Sub-Lieutenant R. A. J. Warneford, in one of the most brilliant aerial exploits of the war—the first Zeppelin brought down by an aeroplane.

Mr. Warneford, who was only 22 years of age, was the son of an Anglo-Indian railway engineer, and before the war was in the mercantile marine. He went home to "do something" for his country, enlisted in the 2nd Sportsman's Battalion, was transferred to the Royal Naval Air Service, passed the tests for a pilot's certificate within a few days, and was given a commission. He was noted at the flying school as one of the most brilliant pupils the instructors had ever known.

A month after obtaining his commission he went to France, where his reckless daring soon made him conspicuous in a service where venture-someness is the general rule. On the morning, of June 7, 1915, at 3 a.m., he encountered a Zeppelin returning from the coast of Flanders to Ghent, and chased it, mounting above it and sailing over it at a height of 6,000 feet. Zeppelin and aeroplane exchanged shots, and when the Zeppelin was between one and two hundred feet immediately below him he dropped six bombs on it. One bomb hit the Zeppelin fairly, causing a terrific explosion, and setting the airship on fire from end to end.

Warneford's aeroplane was caught by the force of the explosion and turned upside down, but he succeeded in righting it before it touched the ground. He was forced to alight within the German lines. Nevertheless, he restarted his engine, though not without great difficulty, and in due course returned to his station without damage. Only the framework of the Zeppelin was left, the crew being all burned or

THE TRAGIC DEATH OF LIEUT. WARNEFORD
A few days after he had destroyed a Zeppelin, he fell to his death while making a flight near Paris. With him Henry Beach Needham, an American writer, was also killed.

mangled, and the body of the machine being completely destroyed. The flaming framework dropped on the Convent School of St. Amandsberg, killing one nun and burning two Sisters who had rushed into the street with children in their arms. The machine on which Warneford made this attack was a *Morane "Parasol,"* a little monoplane with a pair of wings raised well above the pilot's head. This construction gives the aviator full view on either side below, thus enabling him to take good aim for bomb dropping. The *Morane* of that type was also noted as a quick-climbing machine, a very decided advantage in attacking Zeppelins.

The story of Warneford's triumph sent a thrill through England. The king promptly sent a personal telegram of congratulation to him, and conferred upon him the Victoria Cross. The telegram ran as follows:

> I most heartily congratulate you upon your splendid achievement of yesterday, in which you singlehanded destroyed an enemy Zeppelin.
> I have much pleasure in conferring upon you the Victoria Cross for this gallant act.
>
> George R.I.

Next day the French War Minister, on the recommendation of General Joffre, awarded Warneford the Cross of the Legion of Honour. It was known that he was returning on a visit to England. A splendid public welcome was prepared for him. He went first, however, to Paris, and there in company with Henry Needham, an American journalist, he set out on a new Henry Farman biplane, which he proposed to take by air to Dunkirk. Warneford and his passenger had risen to 700 feet when the machine wobbled violently for a few seconds, and then overturned, throwing them both out. They were both killed instantly.

The return to England was different from that which had been anticipated. In the late evening of June 21, a fortnight after the deed which won him fame, the train carrying Warneford's body came into Victoria Station. Thousands of people had assembled there to pay their final tributes to the hero, and the little procession of the coffin covered by the Union Jack, mounted on a gun-carriage, and guarded by seamen of the Royal Naval Division, moved out amid the bared heads of the silent crowd. Warneford was buried in Brompton Cemetery.

The strictly American aviation operations started in the middle of March, 1918, with the patrolling of the front from Villeneuve-les-Ver-

THE PILOT IN THE FORWARD GONDOLA OF A ZEPPELIN
The front gondola of a Zeppelin is screened to protect the pilot and assistants. Searchlights and other means of illumination are carried on board to be used when necessary.

tus by an American pursuit squadron using planes of the French-built Nieuport-28 type. These operations were in the nature of a try-out of the American trained aviators, and their complete success was followed by an immediate increase of the aerial forces at the front, with enlargement of their duties and field of action. By the middle of May, 1918, squadrons of all types—pursuit, observation, and bombing—as well as balloon companies were in operation over a wide front. These squadrons were equipped with the best available types of British and French-built service planes,

One Minute Plus

Three Attacking Hun Machines Downed by "Ricky" in About Seventy Ticks

No one has succeeded better than Boyd Cable, in the *Red Cross Magazine,* in conveying an impression of what "Quick Work" means in the war combats between aeroplanes when the fighting machines are in expert hands. But after all it is doubtful if one can realise in reading how quick the action was, inasmuch as the fight took less time than you will require to read one of these columns aloud. As Mr. Cable says:

> It is difficult, if not indeed impossible, to convey in words what is perhaps the most breath-catching wonder of air-fighting work, the furious speed, the whirling rush, the sheer rapidity of movement of the fighting machines, and the incredible quickness of a pilot's brain, hand, and eye to handle and manoeuvre a machine, and aim and shoot a gun under these speed conditions.
> I can only ask you to try to remember that a modern fast scout is capable of flying at well over a hundred miles an hour on the level, and at double that (one may not be too exact) in certain circumstances, and that in such a fight as I am going to try to describe here the machines were moving at anything between these speeds. If you can bear this in mind, or even realise it—I am speaking to the non-flying reader—you will begin to understand what airmen-o'-war work is, to believe what a pilot once said of air fighting: 'You don't get time to think. If you stop to think, you're dead.'
> When the flight of half a dozen scout machines was getting ready to start on the usual 'offensive patrol' over Hunland, one of the pilots, 'Ricky-Ticky' by popular name, had some slight

trouble with his engine. It was nothing much, a mere reluctance to start up easily, and since he did get her going before the flight was ready to take off, he naturally went up with it. He had a little more trouble in the upward climb to gain a height sufficient for the patrol when it crossed the line to stand the usual respectable chance of successfully dodging the usual 'Archie' shells.

Ricky, however, managed to nurse her up well enough to keep his place in the formation, and was still in place when they started across the lines. Before they were far over Hunland he knew that his engine was missing again occasionally, and was not pulling as she ought to, and from a glance at his indicators and a figuring of speed, height, and engine revolutions was fairly certain that he was going almost full out to keep up with the other machines, which were flying easily and well within their speed.

Following the Chance

This was where he would perhaps have been wise to have thrown up and returned to his 'drome. He hung on in the hope that the engine would pick up again—as engines have an unaccountable way of doing—and even when he found himself dropping back out of place in the formation he still stuck to it and followed on. He knew the risk of this; knew that the straggler, the lame duck, the unsupported machine is just exactly what the Hun flyer is always on the lookout for; knew, too, that his flight-commander before they had started had warned him (seeing the trouble he was having to start up) that if he had any bother in the air or could not keep place in the formation to pull out and return.

Altogether, then, the trouble that swooped down on him was his own fault, and you can blame him for it if you like. But if you do you'll have to blame a good many other pilots who carry on, and in spite of the risk, do their best to put through the job they are on. He finally decided—he looked at the clock fixed in front of him to set a time and found it showed just over one minute to twelve—in one minute, at noon exactly, if his engine had not steadied down to work, he would turn back for home.

At that precise moment—and this was the first warning he had

AIRPLANES IN BATTLE FORMATION
When the first light of day appeared enemy and allied airplanes both ascended and fought for the supremacy of the air.

that there were Huns about—he heard a ferocious rattle of machine gun fire, and got a glimpse of streaking flame and smoke from the tracer bullets whipping past him. The Huns, three of them and all fast fighting scouts, had seen him coming, had probably watched him drop back out of place in the flight, had kept carefully between him and the sun so that his glances round and back had failed to spot them in the glare, and had then dived headlong on him, firing as they came.

They were coming down on him from astern and on his right side, or, as the navals would put it, on his starboard quarter, and they were perhaps a hundred to a hundred and fifty yards off when Ricky first looked round and saw them. His first and most natural impulse was to get clear of the bullets that were spitting round and over him, and in two swift motions he had opened his engine full out, thrust his nose a little down, and was off full pelt.

Promptly the three astern swung a little, opened out as they wheeled, dropped their noses, and came after Ricky, still, a little above him, and so fairly astern that only the centre one could keep a sustained accurate fire on him. (A scout's gun being fixed and shooting between the blades of the propeller—gun and engine being synchronised so as to allow the bullet to pass out as the blade is clear of the muzzle—means that the machine itself must be aimed at the target for the bullets to hit, and two outer machines of the three could only so aim their machines by pointing their noses to converge on the centre one—a risky manoeuvre with machines traveling at somewhere about a hundred miles an hour.)

But the fire of that centre one was too horribly close for endurance, and Ricky knew that although his being end-on made him the smaller target, it also made his machine the more vulnerable to a raking shot which, piercing him fore and aft, could not well fail to hit petrol tank, or engine, or some other vital spot. He could do nothing in the way of shooting back, because, being a single-seater scout himself, his two guns were trained one to shoot straight forward through the propeller, the other, mounted on the top plane on a curved mount allowing the gun to be grasped by the handle above him and pulled back and down, to shoot from direct ahead to straight up? Neither could shoot backward.

Ricky, the first shock of his surprise over, had gauged the situation, and, it must be admitted, it was—

Dangerous if Not Desperate

He had dropped back and back from the flight, until now they were something like a mile ahead of him. A mile, it is true, does not take a modern machine long to cover, but then, on the other hand, neither does an air battle take long to fight, especially with odds of three to one. With those bullets sheeting past him and already beginning to rip and crack through his wings, any second might see the end of Ricky. It was no use thinking longer of running away, and even a straight-down nose-dive offered no chance of escape, both because the Huns could nose-dive after him and continue to keep him under fire, and because he was well over Hunland, and the nearer he went to the ground the better target he would make for the anti-aircraft gunners below. He must act, and act quickly.

A thousand feet down and a quarter of a mile away was a little patch of cloud. Ricky swerved, dipped, and drove 'all out' for it. He was into it—400 yards remember—in about the time it takes you to draw three level quiet breaths, and had flashed through it—five or six hundred feet across it might have been—in a couple of quick heart-beats. The Huns followed close, and in that half-dozen seconds Ricky had something between fifty and a hundred bullets whizzing and ripping past and through his wings.

As he leaped clear of the streaming wisps of the cloud's edge he threw one look behind him and pulled the joy-stick hard in to his stomach. Instantly his machine reared and swooped up in the loop he had decided on, up and over and round. At the first upward zoom Ricky had pulled down the handle of his top gun and brought it into instant action. The result was that as he shot up and over in a perfect loop the centre machine, which had been astern of him, flashed under and straight through the stream of his bullets.

Ricky whirled down in the curve of his loop with his gun still shooting, but now that he had finished his loop and flattened out, shooting up into the empty air while his enemy hurtled straight on and slightly downward ahead of him. Instantly Ricky threw his top gun out of action, and having now reversed positions, and having his enemy ahead, steadied his machine to bring his bow gun sights to bear on her. But before he could fire he saw the hostile's left upper plane twist upward, saw the machine spin side on, the top plane rip and flare fiercely back and upward, the lower plane buckle and break, and the machine turning over and over plunge down and out of his sight. One of his bullets evidently had cut some bracing wires or stays, and the wing had given to the strain upon it. So much Ricky just had time to think, but immediately found himself in a fresh danger.

Clever Work

The two remaining hostiles had flashed past him at the same time as the centre one, while he threw his loop over it, but realizing apparently on the instant what his manoeuvre was, they both swung out and round while he passed in his loop over the centre machine. It was smart work on the part of the two flanking hostiles. They must have instantly divined Ricky's dodge to get astern of them all, and their immediate circle out and round counteracted it, and as he came out of his loop brought them circling in again on him. In an instant Ricky was suddenly roused to the fresh danger by two following short bursts of fire which flashed and flamed athwart him, and caught a glimpse of the other two closing in and again astern of him and 'sitting on his tail.'

Both were firing as they came, and again Ricky felt the sharp rip and crack of explosive bullets striking somewhere on his machine, and an instant later knew that the two were following him and hailing lead upon him. He cursed savagely. He had downed one enemy, but here apparently, he was little if any better off with two intact enemies in the worst possible position for him, 'on his tail,' and both shooting their hardest. A quick glance ahead showed him the white glint of light on the wheeling wings of his flight, attracted by the rattle of machine guns, circling and racing to join the fight.

But fast as they came, the fight was likely to be over before they could arrive, and with the crack and snap of bullets about him and his own two guns powerless to bear on the enemy, it looked uncomfortably like odds on the fight ending against him. Another loop they would expect and follow over—and the bullets were crippling him every instant. Savagely he threw his controls over, and his machine slashed out and down to the right in a slicing two-hundred-foot side-slip.

The right-hand machine whirled past him so close that he saw every detail of the pilot's dress—the fur-fringed helmet, dark goggles, black sweater. He caught his machine out of her downward slide, drove her ahead, steadied her, and brought his sights to bear on the enemy a scant twenty yards ahead, and poured a long burst of fire into her. He saw the bullets break and play on and about the pilot and fuselage.

Then came a leaping flame, and a spurt of black smoke whirling out from her; Ricky had a momentary glimpse of the pilot's agonised expression as he glanced wildly around, and next instant saw a trailing black plume of smoke and the gleam of a white underbody as the enemy nose-dived down in a last desperate attempt to make a landing before his machine dissolved in flames about him.

With a sudden burst of exultation Ricky realised his changed position. A minute before he was in the last and utmost desperate straits, three fast and well-armed adversaries against his single hand. Now, with two down, it was man to man—no, if he wished, it was all over, because the third hostile had swung left, had her nose down, and was 'hare-ing' for home and down toward the covering fire of the German anti-aircraft batteries. Already she was two to three hundred yards away, and the first German Archie soared up and burst with a rending *'Ar-rrgh'* well astern of him. But Ricky's blood was up and singing songs of triumph in his ears. Two out of three downed; better make a clean job of it and bag the lot.

Making A Clean Job

His nose dipped and his tail flicked up, and he went roaring down, full out, after his last Hun. A rapid crackle of one machine gun after another struck his ear before ever he had the last hostile fully centred in his sights. Ricky knew that at last the flight had arrived and were joining in the fight. But he paid no heed to them; his enemy was in the ring of his sights now, so with his machine hurling down at the limit of speed of a falling body plus all the pull of a hundred and odd horsepower, the whole fabric quivering and vibrating under him, the wind roaring past and in his ears, Ricky snuggled closer in his seat, waited till his target was fully and exactly centred in his sights, and poured in a long, clattering burst of fire.

The hostile's slanting nose-dive swerved into a spin, an uncontrolled side-to-side plunge, back again into a spinning dive that ended in a straight-downward rush and a crash end on into the ground.

Whether it was Ricky or some other machine of the flight that got this last hostile will never be known. Ricky himself officially reported having crashed two, but declined to claim the third as his. On the other hand, the rest of the flight, after and always, with enthusiastic unanimity, insisted that she was Ricky's very own, that he had outplayed, outfought, and killed three Huns in single combat with them—one down and t'other come on. If Ricky himself could not fairly and honestly claim all rights to the last Hun, the flight did. '*Three!*' they said vociferously in mess that night, and would brook no modest doubts from him. As the last Hun went reeling down, Ricky, in the official language of the combat reports, 'rejoined formation and continued the patrol.' He pulled the stick toward him and rose buoyantly, knowing that he was holed over and over again, that bullets, and explosive bullets at that, had ripped and rent and torn the fabrics of his machine, possibly had cut away some strut or stay or part of the frame.

But his engine appeared to be all right again, had never misbehaved a moment during the fight, was running now full power and blast; his planes swept smooth and steady along the wind levels, his controls answered exactly to his tender questioning touch. He had fought against odds of three to one and—he had won out. He was safe, barring accident, to land back in his own 'drome; and there were two if not three Huns down on his brazen own within the last—how long?

At the moment of his upward zoom on the conclusion of the fight he glanced at his clock which had not been hit by the enemy fire, could hardly believe what it told him, was only convinced when he recalled that promise to himself to turn back at the end of that minute, and had his belief confirmed by the flight's count of the time between their first hearing shots and their covering the distance to join him. His clock marked exactly noon. The whole fight, from the firing of the first shot

AT THE TOMB OF NAPOLEON
In this historic spot, a hero of the World War,
is being decorated for bravery.

to the falling away of the last Hun, had taken bare seconds over the one minute. That pilot was right; in air fighting 'you don't get time to think.'

THE PICTURES ARE GOOD
That's All That Observation Pilot Miller Cared About When the End Came

Among the men killed at Château Thierry was John Q. Miller, of Fairview, N. C, first lieutenant of the air service, shot down July 24, 1918. He was one of the airmen of whom the public had probably not heard, for his courage and daring were not as spectacular as the bravery of Luke, Rickenbacker or Lufbery. At the time of his death he was the greatest observation pilot on the front, according to the story of Major Elmer R. Haslett in an issue of *United States Air Service*, the official publication of the Army and Navy Air Service Association.

The unsung, silent heroes of the air are the observation pilots, who at the risk of life go forward into impossible places to get pictures of enemy positions and come back with their machines riddled with shrapnel from "archie" fire. At the outset Miller, says Major Haslett, attracted attention for the serious way in which he took his work. He took assignment after assignment when he might have stayed back in the barracks, and never failed to complete his mission. Momentarily driven off by hostile aircraft or by too heavy "archie," he would return to the job and come back with his pictures or observations, and his plane so full of holes that it had to be salvaged.

IN SPITE OF WOUNDS

Six Germans finally brought Miller and his observer down on his last trip over the lines, but not until the photographs had been made. Badly wounded, Miller pulled his plane out of a spin and landed his observer with the pictures. Major Haslett says:

> He gave the plane the gun, and they took off on Johnny's last ride. The plane accompanying was piloted by Lieut. Baker and an observer by the name of Lieut. Jack Lumsden, both of whom were the very finest of our personnel. On this mission Thompson, I believe, was taking photographs—oblique views—which must be taken very low, in fact, dangerously low, in order that the advancing troops may see from the photographs exactly what is in front of them. It was a very poor day, and the clouds were low.
>
> As they were just finishing this perilous work, a drove of eleven

Huns swooped out of the clouds and made for them. Five attacked Lumsden and Baker, and six attacked Thompson and Miller. Our boys were about two or three kilometres within the enemy's lines, and, with such a superiority of numbers, of course, were immediately outclassed.

The Hun planes surrounded Thompson and Miller, pouring in lead from all sides. Thompson, who had shot down a Boche before and had been in a number of scraps, was giving them the fight of his life. Miller was heading toward No Man's Land. It is hard in such a fight to know exactly one's location, and it is better to pick out one's general direction when at such a low altitude, and be sure the plane is on the friendly side of the line before hitting the ground.

While still about a kilometre within German territory, a bullet struck Miller in the chest and another in the arm. Thompson told me that Miller put his hand over the fuselage as if semiconscious, then the plane started to go from right to left, climb and dive as if partly under control.

As Thompson described it, it seemed as if Miller were doing his best to keep up his strength to go on with the flight. They crossed the lines, and as they did so Miller motioned to him in one of his conscious moments as if to point to home. He then put the plane into a dive.

One of the German planes had dropped out of the combat, but the others were determined upon putting the plane down in flames or out of control. In these last few seconds they closed in with every gun concentrated on Miller. This fighting was so close that Thompson was aiming point blank. Miller was shot again; he made some sort of a motion as if falling forward.

Miller's Rallying Feat

In a moment Thompson scored a direct burst into one of the planes; it made a sudden climb, then went into a tail spin from which it never recovered. Thompson swung his *tourrelle* round to get the one coming up on his tail. While himself falling, by sheer good fortune Thompson, fighting to the end, turned loose all he had, and the plane underneath his tail ceased firing, dived and fell within a hundred yards of the other he had just got.

The three remaining Huns followed Miller down. One of them

got Thompson in the arm and leg with an explosive bullet. The plane was out of control. By some miracle, Thompson says, as they were about to strike earth, Miller came out of his forward position, pulled the stick back, and the plane landed without a crash.

Thompson had enough strength to jump out of the cockpit and run around to Miller, who, with a strength that was superhuman, was climbing out of the cockpit, bleeding profusely, his face ghostly white.

He reached his arms up, man-like, and let them rest limply on Thompson's shoulders. With closed eyes, and with a voice barely audible, he mumbled: Thompson, God bless you! They got me, but I got you home, boy—and we brought the pictures back. Get a motorcycle, Tommy, and take them to headquarters. You write a report—I can't, Tommy; you see I can't, Tommy. And be sure to put in it that the pictures are good—that the mission was successful.'

These were his last words, and he fell over unconscious. His wounds were of a hopeless nature, and he died without regaining consciousness a few minutes later in a sort of improvised dressing station in the front lines.

Well, those are incidents in the life of the observation game.

The official records credit Johnny Miller with the destruction of two enemy planes, and the French Government has bestowed upon him posthumously the Croix de Guerre with Palm, but those of us who had the pleasure of serving with him and who have lived to tell the tale credit Johnny Miller with having been just a plain, ordinary, brave fellow, who gave his life with all willingness to insure the successful completion of the mission to which his country assigned him.

SUBDUING THE TURK

When Captain Bott, the British Ace, Found Bakshish a Cure of Captivity

When the war broke out, Alan Bott was one of the younger set of newspaper men in London. Soon after England cast in her lot with France, Bott was training with the airmen. Right speedily he became a fighting flyer and *anon* an Ace, with seven German planes to his credit. He won the Victoria Cross, and the rank of captain. Readers may remember having heard him lecture when he made a tour of this country early in 1919, and gave very impressive pictures of adventures in the air. Not many aviators had the varied experiences that fell to the fortune of Captain Bott, for though he was for a time with his fellows of the Royal British Air Force operating in France, he was transferred to the East later and many of his thrilling adventures were in the Holy Land. He gave an account of one of these soon after his arrival in this country. He said:

> It all began when I fell out of the clouds from a height of six thousand feet and bumped my nose after a fight with a Boche plane. It wasn't exactly a fight with one plane, either. I was chasing a Boche who had a machine nearly as fast as mine, and by the time I caught up with him we were forty miles behind the enemy lines and above some rough, rocky, partly wooded hills. I was just beginning to pepper the Boche when two enemy scout planes I had not seen literally dropped from the clouds right above and shot me up, especially the petrol tank. I whirled and crashed down, and the next thing I knew it was moonlight and my leg was paining like the deuce, held down by part of my engine. It was a very lonely, desert spot, and I figured that hill would be my last resting-place. I figured they would name it after me.
>
> Whether fortunately or not a bunch of Arabs came along, sort of bandits, I suppose, and found me. As far as I could make out, after they lifted the engine off me they were tossing up whether they should kill me or turn me over to the Turks and get some *bakshish*, which is a popular pastime in that part of the country. They used to say that with £1,000 you could bribe the *Grand Vizier* himself.
>
> While they were drawing lots to see whether I would live or die, a party of Turkish soldiers came along and chased the Arabs off, but detained me. In fact, they were decent enough to take me to an Austrian hospital at Afion-Kara-Hisson, about seventy miles from our base at Jaffa. It was three weeks before I could get around much, and then I foolishly tried to escape. My leg was so bad that the attempt was a foozle, as the guards caught me up before I had gone very far.
>
> ### IN JAIL AT NAZARETH
>
> Finally, I was taken to Nazareth and put in a criminal jail with murderers and brigands, all filthy brutes. At first, I was put in an underground dungeon, with one other man, an Arab, whose

great penchant was chasing cooties. There were other English prisoners there, and we were all treated pretty badly. Our food consisted of a bowl of soup and a loaf of bread each day. It was some bread!

Several of us planned to escape and tried several stunts, none of which appealed to the Turks, until I selfishly hit on the scheme of becoming temporarily insane. I was very crazy, for a few days, and then the highly ornate boss of the jail shook his head seriously and said he would have to send me to Constantinople. We finally began to rumble across the desert in a very slow train, and I decided to drop off at the first convenient way-station and cut across lots for Jaffa. We were quite near Constantinople before an opportunity came, and then, at the psychological moment, there was a very opportune train wreck, and I walked away and hid in among some rocks.

When night came I met a Turkish officer dressed in a German uniform, and then worked the popular game of *bakshish*, which is really the national game of Turkey.

I gave the officer a couple of Turkish pounds and he peeled the uniform. He put on mine and I have no doubt he was duly captured by the guards. I went to Constantinople and was saluted very regularly by Turkish and German soldiers. It took a lot of dodging to keep clear of the Germans in Constantinople, but I managed to get along, having a lot of fun sometimes in the *cafés*, listening to the gossip and plotting.

A Stowaway on a "Hell Ship"

It appeared at that time that Turkey had been ready for quite a while to sign a separate peace, but the Allies couldn't get the idea. My greatest desire was to get out of Constantinople, and I finally stowed away on a little rusty cargo-steamer bound for Odessa. We were rolling around the Black Sea one day when the crew were seized with Bolshevism and went on strike.

It was great on that ship with the engines dead. We rolled and rolled for days on end. I had bought a Russian sailor's uniform by that time and so could go about without fear of capture. The main thing was to get a crust of bread and cup of water. It was a hell ship and no mistake, with the sun beating down all day and the officers and crew in continual fights.

Finally, they patched up a truce and we made Odessa, the trip taking almost three weeks. It was bad in Odessa and when we heard that Bulgaria had made a separate peace I decided to make a try for the Bulgarian coast. I stowed away aboard another cargo steamship and finally reached Bulgaria and my British countrymen.

A Daring Pursuit

In an Ordinary Plane Aviator Bone Chased a German Sea-Plane Over Sea

On Sunday, March 19, 1916, four German sea-planes sailed over East Kent, England, in a bombing raid upon defenceless towns—Deal, Margate, Ramsgate—and arrived over Dover about 2 o'clock in the afternoon and dropped more than a dozen bombs, doing a considerable amount of damage. One bomb went through the roof of a Home where there were a large number of children; fortunately, the children, at the first sound of the raiders, had been taken to the shelter of the basement. Several children going to Sunday school were killed or injured. A woman walking along the street was blown into a doorway of a shop and badly hurt.

The invaders were given very little time to do their work. British aeroplanes rose in pursuit. A sharp fight followed, both attackers and defenders using their machine guns freely in the air. One British airman particularly distinguished himself. Flight Commander R. J. Bone, R. N., pursued one of the German seaplanes out to sea for nearly 30 miles, in a small single-seater land machine. There, after an engagement lasting about a quarter of an hour, he forced it to descend, the German machine having been hit many times, and the observer disabled or killed. For this, Flight Commander Bone received the D. S. O.

The commander left the aerodrome while the enemy machine was still in sight, and making no attempt to climb steeply, kept the enemy in view. After a pursuit of nearly 30 miles he rose to 9,000 feet, 2,000 feet above the enemy. Rapidly overhauling the other machine, he attempted to make a vertical dive for it, both sides firing vigorously. Then he manoeuvred ahead of the other and steered straight at him, diving below him and turning with a vertical right-hand bank immediately under him.

Brought Him Down

The German pilot swerved his machine to the left before they met, and the Englishman as he passed could see the German observer hanging over the right side of the fuselage, apparently dead or severely wounded. The gun was cocked at an angle of 45 degrees. Continuing his courageous manoeuvre's, Flight-Commander Bone brought his machine within 15 or 20 feet of the enemy, and poured in five or six bursts of six rounds until the enemy dived deeply, with smoke pouring from his machine. The propeller stopped, but the pilot kept control and succeeded in landing safely on the water. Here the English airman had to leave him, as he could not come down on a land machine, and his engine showed signs of giving out.

One machine apparently escaped from the fight at Dover and rapidly made its way to Deal, where it dropped seven bombs, doing considerable damage to property, but not killing or injuring any persons. A second pair of sea-planes appeared over Ramsgate at 2.10 p.m. and dropped bombs on the town. Four children on their way to Sunday school were killed, and a man driving a motorcar nearby was also killed. A hospital for Canadian troops was damaged, but no one in the building was hurt, and the nurses went out in the streets to assist in the work of tending the injured. One of the sea-planes travelled on from Ramsgate to Margate, where it dropped a bomb, damaging a house. The German aircraft were now all pursued by British machines and driven out to sea.

THE ROOSEVELT BOYS

Four Sons of a Famous Fighter Gather Their Own Laurels of War

The Roosevelts are not the only family to have given four sons to the cause of their country, and those other sons have fought as bravely as Archibald and Theodore and Kermit, and died as daringly as Quentin. It isn't, then, because the sacrifices of the Roosevelts are unique that they have become so dear to the hearts of Americans. The Roosevelts would be the first to decry any attempt to single out their deeds as any nobler than the deeds of their millions of comrades in arms.

It seems only fair, however, to the traditions of our democracy that having recounted so many exploits by heroes who before the war were not known outside their little towns, we should include a few of the many, many names which proved that connection with more noted families did not make them any slower to welcome the dangers which war brought alike to rich and poor.

ARCHIE GOES TO FRANCE

Back in June, 1917, Theodore Roosevelt, Jr., went across with Ar-

THEODORE ROOSEVELT
The late Ex-President of the United States,
and great American Patriot.

THEODORE ROOSEVELT AND FAMILY
AT THE TIME HE WAS GOVERNOR OF THE STATE OF NEW YORK

chie. Theodore was a major then; Archie a captain. Both were assigned to General Pershing's staff. In August, it was reported that the two, anxious for real action, had been transferred to the 26th Infantry. So anxious was Archie to get into line duty that he accepted a reduction to Second Lieutenancy in order to get into the trenches.

All this had happened quickly. It was only in April that Archie had been engaged to Grace Lockwood. Some five days after that he had passed his examination for the Officers' Reserve Corps. By April 15 he had married. June 20, he left Plattsburg with confidential orders. June 25 his father announced that Archie and Theodore had left for France.

Archie did not stay long as a Second Lieutenant. By Christmas, following distinguished service in leading patrols in No Man's Land, General Pershing recommended that Archie be promoted. In February Archie was made a captain. One month later Captain Archie was wounded in the arm and leg by hrapnel. He received the French War Cross while lying on the operating table. "He lay wounded for fourteen hours unattended," writes an American surgeon in a letter home, lit May Archie was reported able to walk again.

His wounds did not make Archie callous to the suffering of others. In July (1918) we read that:

> Archie's request for aid for Sergeant F. A. Ross whose hand was amputated will be heeded by Colonel Roosevelt.

A shrapnel wound of its nature usually results in more serious complications than an ordinary bullet wound. On July 13, the captain had to undergo another operation for partial paralysis of the left arm. His spirit never wavered. When wounded he had directed that the wounded men in his command be attended first. Archie was hurt worse than he knew. It would take eight months, at least, for him to recover. In September, he was brought back to the United States for special treatment.

THEODORE, THE IDOL OF HIS MEN

In the meantime, Theodore was making himself feared, loved and famous. He was a major, we said. He had been a major once before, but under what different conditions—a Major in the Connecticut National Guards. He got into action from the very start. You could find him at the head of the most dangerous charges. In June (1918) he was cited for bravery after he had been gassed in the fight at Cantigny.

CAPTAIN ARCHIE ROOSEVELT ON FIFTH AVENUE IN NEW YORK. HE WAS WOUNDED IN ACTION.

(FORMERLY) COLONEL THEODORE ROOSEVELT, JUNIOR. He was gassed in the fight at Cantigny, and wounded when making a charge at Ploisy.

(PROMOTED) LIEUTENANT-COLONEL THEODORE ROOSEVELT, JR.

Theodore, too, retained his tenderness despite war's horrors. In July, we read of his paying homage to Lieut. G. Gustofson, Jr. In September, he writes to the widow of Lieut. Newbold telling her that he would be proud to have his two little sons grow up to live and die like the lieutenant. Theodore's men made an idol of him. That, however, did not save him a second wound—this time (July 24) it was in the left knee. He received it while leading a battalion in a charge at Ploisy. It was the same fearlessness which a month before had called forth the official citation.

> On the day of our attack on Cantigny, although gassed in the lungs and gassed in the eyes to blindness, Major Roosevelt refused to be removed and retained the command of his battalion under a heavy bombardment throughout the engagement.

After his second operation, Major Roosevelt was promoted once more, and it was as lieutenant-colonel that in November he occupied the headquarters of von Hindenburg's son at Luxemburg.

Kermit in Mesopotamia and France

The major's younger brother Kermit had, like the rest, come in from the very start, but fortune kept at least this one member of the family a little safer. He had left Plattsburg to accept a position in the British Army as early as July, 1917. In September, he was made Temporary Honorary Captain. After being rewarded with the Distinguished Service Order for bravery with the British in Mesopotamia, Kermit, through the aid of Lord Derby, obtained a transfer to the American Army. In April, he was appointed Captain.

By June he had received the British Military Cross.

Quentin

Kermit, Archibald, Theodore—all have done their duty, but, of course, death has made the youngest of the Roosevelts dearest to American hearts. Perhaps, indeed, the death of no other man at the front has so touched the people as that of young Lieutenant Quentin. He stands almost like the symbol of young America giving itself up for freedom. The *Outlook* writes:

> In the sorrow of his parents, his fellow-countrymen have felt the sorrow of all who have lost sons in this struggle. In the pride, his parents have simply expressed his fellow-countrymen have been able to understand in part the pride of all those who

CAPTAIN KERMIT ROOSEVELT

have learned that for his purpose of making mankind free God has had need of their dearest. In honouring Quentin Roosevelt Americans honour all those young men who have rendered to their country their full measure of devotion.

Part of the special glory of the Roosevelts comes from the fact that they were watched so closely. Quentin, especially, was known to the nation from his very childhood. The nation knew him, and it watched him. Quentin died fighting against odds—a symbol of young American manhood. (Quentin Roosevelt's story by Kermit Roosevelt is published by Leonaur in *Eagles Rampant Rising,* which also contains Charles J. Biddle's book *The Way of the Eagle).*

When we think of what Colonel Roosevelt and his sons stood for in this war there is something soul-stirring in the fact that the father and his youngest boy have both so suddenly passed away, and in the light of all this there is a pathetic significance in the answer which Colonel Roosevelt gave to the man who at a public meeting asked the colonel why he himself had not gone across:

> I asked not only to go over there, but I came with one hundred thousand more men in my hands to help. And I will tell you, you man over there, that I have sent my four sons. I have sent over my four boys, for each of whose lives I care a thousand times more than I care for my own.

Of these four sons Kermit received his cross for bravery. Archibald and Theodore rose steadily from rank to rank—wounds and honour marking their path. And Quentin gave his life. There is something more than fortitude in the words of the proud, strong, old man bearing up against the saddest of tidings:

> Quentin's mother and I are very glad he got to the front and had the chance to render some service to his country, and to show the stuff there was in him before his fate befell him.

Quentin Roosevelt was not yet twenty-one. He was born in Washington, November 19, 1897, while his father was Assistant Secretary of the Navy. After 1901 Quentin, starting out as the "White House baby," kept Washington interested and amused for seven years.

Sturdy, impetuous, frank, and democratic, he was friends with everybody. He rode locomotives between Washington and Philadelphia with his chums, the engineers and firemen of the Baltimore & Ohio and the Pennsylvania.

QUENTIN ROOSEVELT'S ENTRANCE CARD
INTO THE *ECOLE DE TIR AERIEN*

FACSIMILE OF QUENTIN ROOSEVELT'S RECORD CARD
IN THE *ECOLE DE AERIEN DE CASUAZ*.
The captain's remarks at the bottom of the card: "Very good pilot; regular landings; very good shot; excellent military spirit, and very daring."

Meantime, he was captain also of a crew of warrior Indians recruited from members of his classes in a public school.

One day, during an illness of his brother Archie, Quentin decided that a sight of a pet pony might prove better than the White House doctor's prescriptions.

Without waiting for permission, he went out to the stables, introduced the Shetland into one of the private elevators, and had the little horse on the way into his sick brother's room before he was stopped.

As recorded by the *New York Times*:

> Quentin's life while in Washington—he was running around here in kilts and afterward in short trousers when his father was President—was just the adventurous childhood of the boy who later slammed his motorcycle into a tree at Oyster Bay when he was trying to establish a new speed record and smiled when a home-assembled automobile took a corner under his guidance on one wheel. He was not afraid for himself and worried only about the expense of rebuilding the motorcycle.

Quentin was sent to Harvard. He took a prominent part in athletics. He inherited his father's pluck and determination. Like his father, too, Quentin suffered from a defect of vision. That is why when the first officers training-camp was organised and Archie was admitted and won a commission, Quentin, on account of his eyes, was rejected.

He thereupon applied for enlistment in the Canadian Flying Corps. That was in April, 1917. When the United States decided to send troops to Europe he was transferred to the United States Signal Corps as a private.

He underwent a brief period of training at Mineola. He reached France a few weeks after Archie, who, we remember, was then a captain. Theodore, Jr., was already commanding one of the first American battalions to go under fire. Kermit also had by that time sailed for the war zone.

He Makes a Down

Quentin became known to his fellow flyers as "Q." Before the fatal day he had been fighting in the air five weeks. A few days before that last fight Quentin had a very narrow escape. He was cut off by a cloud from his fellows and coming out of the clouds saw three aviators whom he took for Americans. When he got quite close he found they were Boches, and coolly opened fire on them. All three attacked him.

LIEUTENANT QUENTIN ROOSEVELT

Quentin "did" for one of them and got home safe. An account of this is included in Captain McLanahan's description of Quentin's last days.

> Our airdrome was north of Verdun, about twenty miles back of the American front line. Quentin had joined us June 1. He had been instructor at the aviation school at Issoudun, and I had formed his acquaintance there. I left Issoudun for patrol work at the front about two months before Quentin was allowed to join us. They liked his work at the aviation school so well that he had a hard time to obtain leave to get into the more perilous work at the front, for which he was always longing.
> Our regular occupation in the patrol service consisted of two flights a day, each lasting from an hour and a half to two hours. As this involved the necessity of going over the enemy lines, it was, of course, extremely trying upon the nerves. I doubt whether anybody, except perhaps the most foolhardy, ever performed this sort of work without feeling greatly exhausted after a few hours of so tense a strain. Nevertheless, we were often required, when circumstances demanded it, to go aloft four or even more times in the course of a day. This was of rare occurrence and only when the enemy showed extreme activity and every resource at our command had to be called into service in opposition.
> Usually a patrol consisted of three squads of from six to eight planes, one squad going to a height of 20,000 feet, the second 12,000, and the third 4,000 feet. They would fly in V formation, the leader about a hundred feet below the level of the next two, these 100 feet lower than those next after them, and so on to the last ones of the squad, who were always the highest.

July 14 was an exceptionally fine day for the sort of work the squadron was doing. "We went up at eleven o'clock in the forenoon," says Captain McLanahan, and describes the flight and the fatal fight that followed:

> There were eight of us, all, at that time, Lieutenants—Curtis, of Rochester, N.Y.; Sewall, of Bath, Me.; Mitchell, of Manchester, Mass.; Buford, of Nashville, Tenn.; Roosevelt, Hamilton, Montague, and I. As was customary, we chatted together before we went up, and of course, planned what we were going to do. It was arranged that Lieutenant Hamilton was to lead, and in case of any hitch to his motor Lieutenant Curtis was to take his

place in the van.

There was a rather stiff wind blowing in the direction of the German lines, and when we reached an altitude of about 10,000 feet we began to be carried with great rapidity toward them. We had not yet sighted any enemy airplanes after we had been aloft an hour. Hamilton's motor went wrong about that time and he had to glide back home. In a few minutes, he was followed by Montague, whose motor also had gone back on him.

Meeting the Enemy

Half an hour after this, when we were five miles inside the German lines, we saw six of their *Fokker* planes coming toward us. They had been concealed until then by clouds between them and us, they flying on the underside of the clouds. Our planes were of the Nieuport type, of the lightest pursuing kind, and in almost every respect like the type the Germans approaching us were using. The chief difference was that they carried stationary motors while ours were rotary ones, which gave us a trifle the advantage in turning. But this was more than neutralised by the very much greater inflammable material in our machines.

When we got to within 500 feet of each other both sides began firing. The weapons on each side were virtually identical, each Nieuport and each *Fokker* carrying two machine guns. As each plane had but one occupant, upon whom, of course, devolved the work not only of steering his craft but firing the guns, there was an arrangement by which these two duties could be executed with, so to speak, one movement. The steering-gear and the firing and aiming devices were adjusted to a stick in front of the aviator, in such a manner that his hand could clutch all three levers at once and work each by a slight pressure.

Each of the machine guns carried about 250 rounds of ammunition, and unless it got jammed it was capable of firing the entire lot in half a minute. In order to determine whether the aim is accurate some of the bullets are so constructed that they emit smoke and can thus be seen. These are called tracers. Without them it would be well-nigh impossible to gage one's range so far up in the air, remote from anything by which comparisons could be made to rectify the judgment in aiming.

From the moment that I singled out the enemy whom I was to engage in duel I naturally lost sight of everything else and kept my eyes pretty well glued upon him alone. Now and then, of course, I would, when I got a chance, look backward, too. For one can never tell but that another enemy plane, having disposed of its opponent, may pay his respects to another one.

But if anybody imagines that an aviator engaged in battle with an active opponent gets a chance to help along an associate, or even to pay attention to what is happening to any of the others, he is mistaken. One has to be on the alert for every move the enemy makes, and even do a lot of correct guessing as to what would be the most logical next move for him to make. For it is upon that next move that the entire fortunes of the war for those particular two aviators may hinge.

After I had fired every round of ammunition, which seemed to be about the same time as my adversary discovered himself to be in the same plight, we drew away from each other and flew toward our respective bases. During our duel, my airplane had become separated from the others of our unit and I could see no trace of them. I assumed, however, that they were either still fighting or had also finished and were on their way back home. Somehow, I did not think of the third alternative, namely, that anything serious had happened to any of them.

Indeed, one's thoughts are so completely directed toward the business in hand, especially during a fight, that there is not a moment's time that can be devoted to other matters, even those of the dearest, tenderest, or most sacred nature. To divert the mind even for an instant from the grim business of battle itself would be scarcely short of suicidal. And the home-bound journey after the battle is enlivened by so continuous a gauntlet of bursting enemy anti-aircraft shells that they suffice to keep the mind engaged in ways and means of dodging them until the home base is finally reached. During an air-battle, of course, the anti-aircraft guns are silent, for their shells would be equally dangerous for friend and foe.

All but Quentin Returned

Lieutenants Buford and McLanahan arrived after all of the others, except Lieutenant Roosevelt, had returned to the field. They were not worried about him at the time, but when hours went by and he failed to return, they knew that something had gone wrong. Still, they did not think he had been killed. As Captain McLanahan explains:

We were encouraged to hope for the best by the fact that Quentin had remained out a considerable time longer than the rest of us three days before. On that occasion, he had become separated from the squad, I don't just know in what way, and when we saw him again he jumped out of his airplane in great excitement and so radiant with elation and with so broad a smile that his teeth showed exactly in the same famous way as his father's used to do. He never reminded us so much of his father as on that occasion.

He told us that after losing track of us he sighted a group of airplanes which he believed to be ours and headed his airplane toward them. He was too cautious, however, to take anything for granted, and so in steering toward the group he kept himself in the rear of them, and when he got closer he discovered that they had the cross of the Germans painted on them.

His first impulse was to get away as fast as possible; but then the hero in him spoke up and he decided to avail himself of the chance to reduce the number of our enemies by at least one. And so, flying quite close to the last one of the airplanes, he fired quickly and with such good aim that the plane immediately went down, spinning around, with its nose pointed to the ground.

'I guess I got that one all right,' he said; but he did not wait to see what the final outcome might be, for aviators are full of tricks and, by feigning disaster to their own machine, often succeeded in drawing an overconfident enemy to destruction. Quentin knew this; and moreover, he had another big contract on his hands, namely, to get away from the associates of the man whom he had attacked. They all turned upon him, firing from a dozen machine guns; but in firing his own gun he had wheeled about at the same instant, and in that way had a big handicap over the pursuers. He kept far enough in advance of them to get back within the American lines before they were able to lessen the distance sufficiently to make their shells effective. The rate of speed, by the way, was 140 miles an hour.

Despite his excitement and the really exceptional achievement, Quentin modestly refrained from declaring positively that he had bagged his man. It was only afterward, when we learned through an artillery observation-balloon that the airplane brought down by Quentin had been seen to strike the earth with a crash, that he himself felt satisfied that he was entitled to be regarded the victor. This was the occasion which brought him the *Croix de Guerre*.

When the day passed and Quentin failed to return, his associates still remained hopeful that he had landed in the enemy lines, and had been taken prisoner. But there was further news, bad news, as Captain McLanahan relates:

> Even this forlorn hope was dispelled the following day, when news was received that an observation-balloon's crew had seen a Nieuport machine fall at Chamery, east of Fère-en-Tardenois, the place where Quentin had gone into the battle.
>
> ### Germans Report Death
>
> A few days after that German aviators flying over the American lines dropped notes announcing that Lieut. Quentin Roosevelt had been killed by two bullet wounds in the head and had been buried with military honours by the Germans.
> After the armistice was signed, we saw the aviator who had killed Quentin. He was a non-commissioned officer and one of the most expert flyers in the enemy's air service. After the armistice, he was acting as an inspector in the surrender of German airplanes to the Allies.
> This man said that when he learned that the officer whom he had brought down belonged to so prominent a family in America he felt sorry.
> 'He was identified by a metal identification-plate fastened by a little chain to his wrist,' said the German, 'and I was then told of the young man's prominence and his own personal popularity. Of course, even if I had known during the battle who he was, I would not have hesitated to try my best to down him; because, if I hadn't, he surely would have downed me.
> 'He made a gallant fight, although I recognised almost from the beginning of our duel that he was not as experienced as some others I had encountered and won out against.
> 'As it was, he dipped and circled and looped and tried in a variety of ways to get above and behind me. It was not at all an easy task for me to get the upper hand and down him.'

Simple praise this is, but sincere we feel. The German felt sorry for our boy-hero. "He made a gallant fight," he said. And he was not the

WHEN THE GREAT AMERICAN PATRIOT DIED FLYERS DROPPED WREATHS FROM THE AIR OVER THE ROOSEVELT HOME AT SAGAMORE HILL

only German who was forced to give due admiration to the dauntless American. The enemy buried him with military honours, and marked his grave. The German Cross, however, has been removed from the grave of Quentin. The grave is now simply fenced with stones. The French strew flowers over it. It bears a soldier's inscription:

> Here rests on the field of honor First Lieutenant Quentin Roosevelt, killed in action July, 1918.

A memorial just as eloquent in its simplicity is the letter from General Pershing to the father of Quentin:

> Lieutenant Quentin Roosevelt during his whole career in the air service both as a cadet and as a flying officer was a model of the best type of young American manhood.

Quentin is a hero— a soldier—an officer—yet most of all he remains to our memory as our ex-President's youngest boy. Eleanor Reed expresses this lasting appeal in her poem to Quentin, in the New York *Times*:

> *Young Roosevelt is dead—and I whose son*
> *Is just a little boy, too young to go,*
> *Read with bewildered eyes the tales recalled*
> *Of pranks the little White House boy had played.*

Just What He Wanted

A Restless Seeker After Excitement, the War Filled the Bill for Lieutenant Roberts

Few young men enlisted for the war more frankly in the spirit of adventure than did Lieutenant E. M. Roberts, an American boy, born in Duluth, and seemingly born with the unrest of the winds of the Northwest in his blood. When he was but ten years old he ran away from home in obedience to the restless longing to fare for himself, go whither he listed, and taste the ruggedness of nature in experience. He tried lumbering in the Northwest. He crossed the border into Canada and successively turned his hand to many things—mining, automobile repair, railroad construction, cow-punching, sheep-raising, etc.—getting a liberal education in the "University of Hard Knocks," as he expressed it, but never finding just the excitement he vaguely yearned for.

He was in Calgary in October, 1914, and by chance learned from a newspaper in which he had wrapped a purchase, that there was war doing in Europe. It struck him that the thing sought, the desired excitement, was now ready to hand. He met an old friend and talked the news with him. The friend told him that there had been a call that morning for men for service in Europe. "Let's join!" Both were of the same mind; both were ready for adventure. Next morning, he enlisted as a member of the 10th Canadian Infantry Battalion. But the officer in charge of the barracks knew Roberts, and recalling that he was familiar with mechanics, transferred him to a mechanical transport section, not at all to his liking, mechanics being but a tame affair.

In time, he went with the battalion to France as driver of a lorry. He got a dose of gas at Ypres and was sent back to England for hospital treatment. On recovery, he was returned to France as Section Sergeant, his duty being to scout the roads ahead on a motorcycle. He found that he was getting very little out of the war but hard work, plodding knee deep in mud much of the time while up there the flyers were having a jolly, enviable time.

Ambition to get into the Royal Flying Corps seized him and never let go of him, but it was long before the opportunity to join came to him. Much experience of many kinds came his way, despatch riding among the rest, before the happy day when he was attached to an air squadron as gunner on probation, the getting of which position was in itself an adventure, as is duly set forth in *A Flying Fighter*, the intensely interesting story of his career told by Roberts himself.

Though on the way he was yet far from his goal. He had first to go into the trenches to learn what infantrymen had to go through. He got a thorough lesson, which included prowls in No Man's Land, charging enemy trenches and plunging in to prod with the bayonet and fling hand grenades and much like matter rather adapted, one would imagine, to disqualify an aspirant for service in the air, for rising above ground. But he arrived in due time at the dignity of an accepted aviator, and made his first flight. Then came the excitement of shooting down his first Hun, but we pass that and many other arresting incidents and exploits of his apprenticeship to come to his account of an exceptional sort of encounter with hostile planes that has in it all the elements of dramatic surprise.

He was assigned to pilot duty with a scout and fighting squadron doing service in France, and his first turn of service consisted of patrol duty for three days running. It was an uneventful start, nothing occurring in the three days. On the fourth day, he went up again on patrol to 20,000 feet. He was looking for Huns up there but found none.

As it was very cold he decided to go down a way, and shut off power. He says:

> At the level of 18,000 feet, I found myself sweeping along a very large peak of cloud. Intending to spoil its pretty formation I dived into it, and coming out on the other side, found myself alongside of a Hun plane of the Albatross type. (Roberts was in a Spad.) I had no intimation at all that a Hun was present, and I guess he was in the same position.
>
> ### "The Hun Waved at Me and I Waved at Him"
>
> I suppose he was as much surprised as I was when he saw me emerging from the cloud. Neither of us could shoot at the other for the reason that the guns of the machines we were flying were fixed to the machine so that the machine itself has to be pointed.
>
> We were so close together that this could not be done without our ramming one another, which both of us had to avoid if we did not wish to crash to the earth together.
>
> The Hun waved at me and I waved at him.
>
> We found ourselves in a very peculiar situation. I was so close to him that I could see with the naked eye every detail of his machine. His face also I could see quite clearly, even to the wrinkles around his mouth.
>
> There was something odd in our position. I had to smile at the thought that we were so close together and yet dared not harm one another. The Hun also smiled. Then I reached down to feel the handle on my pressure reservoir to make sure that it was in its proper place, for I knew that one of us would soon have to make a break.
>
> I had never before met a Hun at such close quarters in the air and though we flew parallel to one another for only a few minutes, the time seemed like a week. I remembered some of the tactics told me by some of the older and best fighters in the corps, and was wondering how I could employ them. Finally, a thought occurred to me. Two machines flying at the same height are not necessarily on exactly the same level, as they keep going up and down for about 20 feet.
>
> I was flying between the Hun and his own lines and I had fuel for another hour and a quarter anyway. I wanted to make sure of this bird, but decided to play a waiting game. We continued

our flight side by side.

After a while, however, much sooner than I expected, the Hun began to get restless and started to manoeuvre for position; like myself he was utilising the veriest fraction of every little opportunity in his endeavour to outmanoeuvre the antagonist. Finally, the Hun thought he had gotten the lead.

I noticed that he was trying to side-slip, go down a little, evidently for the purpose of shooting me from underneath, but not far enough for me to get a dive on him. I was not quite sure as yet that such was really his intention, but the man was quick. Before I knew what had happened he had managed to put five shots into my machine, but all of them missed me.

The Hun Spins Earthward

I manoeuvred into an offensive position as quickly as I could, and before the Hun could fire again I had my machine gun pelting him. My judgment must have been fairly good.

The Hun began to spin earthward. I followed to finish him, keeping in mind, meanwhile, that it is an old game in flying to let the other man think you are hit. This bit of strategy will often give an opportunity to get into a position that will give you the drop on your antagonist. The ruse is also sometimes used to get out of a fight when in trouble with gun jam, or when bothered by a defective motor.

I discovered soon that this precaution was not necessary, for the Hun kept spinning down to the ground. He landed with a crash.

A few minutes later I landed two fields away from the wreck and ran over to see the kill I had made.

I had hit the Hun about fifty times and had nearly cut off both his legs at the hips.

There was nothing left in the line of souvenirs, as the Tommies had gotten to the wreck before I did. I carried off a piece of his props and had a stick made of it. That night we had a celebration over the first Hun I had brought down behind our own line since I became a pilot.

Next day I went out to get another Hun to add to my collection. I was in the act of crossing the Hun lines when, *bang!* to the right of me came a thud, and my engine stopped. Revenge, I thought. I volplaned to the ground, made a good landing in a field just behind our lines, and, 'phoning up the squad, I then had another engine brought out to replace mine.

AVIATOR PRICE DOWNS THREE PLANES

On my way to the squadron I witnessed one of the greatest air fights I have ever seen. It took place above the cemetery of P——.

Three Huns were aloft behind their own lines, and back of them was one of our patrolling scouts.

The Hun does not believe in coming over our lines if he can possibly help it, and generally he will manoeuvre so that any engagement will have to be waged over German territory.

One of our men named Price, who was coming in from patrol, was pilot of the scout, which was; flying at the same height as the Hun aircraft, about 12,000 feet. Price was well behind the Hun lines when they saw him, and all three of them made for him at once. I happened to be at an artillery observation post, which I had to pass on my way home, and so was able to get a good view of the combat.

The foremost of the Huns made straight for Price, and for a minute it looked as though he intended ramming him. The combatants separated again and began to fire upon one another, as the tut-tut-tut of the machine guns told me. Of a sudden one Hun volplaned, while another made straight for Price. I wondered what Price would do, but saw the next moment that he had 'zoomed' over the second Hun machine, which just then swooped down upon him. While Price was 'zooming' I noticed that the first Hun was falling to the ground, having either been disabled or killed by Price's machine gun.

Yet within a few moments the second Hun also crashed to earth, and the third was now making for home as fast as his motor would carry him; but Price chased and quickly caught up with him. It was an exciting race. Price was working his machine gun for all the thing was worth, and before long the third Hun went down.

Just five minutes had been required for the fight. When I met Price later I congratulated him. I remember wishing him all the good luck a fellow could have. But that did not help, for within a month he, too, came down in a heap.

Roberts won his lieutenant's commission and achieved the distinction of Ace before he returned home. He was four times wounded in mid-air.

******

In April, 1918, the American forces just going into active sectors had three squadrons, two for observation and one for pursuit. Their strength totalled 35 planes. In May, 1918, the squadrons were increased to nine. The most rapid growth occurred after July, 1918, when American De Haviland planes were becoming available in quantity for observation and day bombing service, and by November, 1918, the number of squadrons increased to 45, with a total of 740 planes in action.

THE RED BATTLE FLYER

Von Richthofen's Brilliant Career in the Air an Offset to His Failure as a Uhlan

The cheery egotism of a man fully assured within himself that he merits his own good opinion is the dominant note of Captain Baron Manfred Freiherr von Richthofen's account of his experiences as a flyer. It is not an offensive egotism; you do not resent it; though you may smile, wondering that a spirit so entirely valiant could so lock arms with that quality of juvenile vanity commonly described as "cockiness." Von Richthofen was a remarkable fellow, the most debonair as well as the most redoubtable of the German aviators and really entitled to exemption from the opprobrious terms of "Hun" and "Boche."

Though a resolute foe he did not forget that he was a gentleman, an aristocrat, and he played the game on that level. He was easily the foremost of aviators—as far as official recognition can determine priority—at the time of his death, April 21, 1918. He then had a record of 80 downs—70 aeroplanes and 10 observation balloons. His nearest rival at that time was Major Raymond Collishaw, the British Ace, with a record of 77.

Von Richthofen was shot down on the Amiens front, over the Somme, April 21st, and his machine, a new and elaborate tri-plane of the *Fokker* type, recently presented to him—its speed was 140 miles an hour and it could climb 15,000 feet in 17 minutes—fell in the British lines. The esteem in which he was held by those who had so often sought to shoot him down was attested in his burial with full military honours and the tributes of genuine admiration heaped on his grave. In the fifteen months of his active flying he became the favourite of the *Kaiser* and the idol of the Germany Army. Someone has said, perhaps not too extravagantly, that the fall of Amiens, then besieged, would not have compensated Germany for the loss she sustained in the death of the greatest and most beloved of her heroes of the air.

Von Richthofen belonged to the country gentry, of noble family. He entered the Cadet Corps when he was eleven years old. In 1911, he entered the army. At the outbreak of the war he was a lieutenant of Uhlans. He went to the Western front with his regiment. His first experience with whistling bullets was when he and his company of Uhlans, out to ascertain the strength of the enemy in the forest near Virton, were caught in a trap. They fled in wild disorder, not without casualties. He was in the trenches before Verdun and found it "boresome." When off duty he sought amusement shooting game in the forest of La Chaussee. So passed several months. Then one day he rebelled against inactivity. It was not the thing for which he went to war. He made his plea to the higher powers. With much grumbling, his prayer was granted. He joined the Flying Service in May, 1915. He made his first flight the next day as an observer. Of that experience, he wrote in his book:

His First Flight

The draft from the propeller was a beastly nuisance. I found it quite impossible to make myself understood by the pilot. Everything was carried away by the wind. If I took up a piece of paper it disappeared. My safety helmet slid off. My muffler dropped off. My jacket was not sufficiently buttoned. In short, I felt very uncomfortable. Before I knew what was happening, the pilot went ahead at full speed and the machine started rolling. We went faster and faster. I clutched the sides of the car. Suddenly, the shaking was over, the machine was in the air and the earth dropped away from under me.

I had been told the name of the place to which we were to fly. I was to direct my pilot. At first, we flew right ahead, then my pilot turned to the right, then to the left, but I had lost all sense of direction above our own aerodrome. I had not the slightest notion where I was!

He continued—with steadily increasing knowledge of aircraft—to serve as an observer until October 10, 1915, when, having passed his examination and been accepted as a pilot, he had the ecstasy of his first solo-flight. In his book (*The Red Battle Flyer,*—republished by Leonaur in *Richthofen & Böelcke in Their Own Words* along with *An Aviator's*

Field Book by Oswald Böelcke), he describes that flight:

> I started the machine. The aeroplane went at the prescribed speed and I could not help noticing that I was actually flying. After all I did not feel timorous but rather elated. I did not care for anything. I should not have been frightened no matter what happened. With contempt of death I made a large curve to the left, stopped the machine near a tree, exactly where I had been ordered to, and looked forward to see what would happen.
> Now came the most difficult thing, the landing. I remembered exactly what movements I had to make. I acted mechanically and the machine moved quite differently from what I had expected. I lost my balance, made some wrong movements, stood on my head and I succeeded in converting my aeroplane into a battered school 'bus. I was very sad, looked at the damage which I had done to the machine, which after all was not very great, and had to suffer from other people's jokes.
> Two days later I went with passion at the flying and suddenly I could handle the apparatus.

The Böelcke Circus

It was not, however, until September 17, 1915, when he was a member of the newly organised Böelcke flying squadron that came to be known as the Circus, that he scored his "first English victim." It was "a gloriously fine day, and therefore only to be expected that the English would be very active," so under the leadership of Böelcke the squadron took the air. As they approached the front, Böelcke discovered an Allied squadron going in the direction of Cambrai. There were seven of the Allies to five of the Germans. They came within range. Here is a sample of that "cockiness" with which von Richthofen described his various and manifold encounters:

> The Englishman nearest to me was traveling in a large boat painted with dark colours. I did not reflect very long but took my aim and shot. He also fired and so did I, and both of us missed our aim. A struggle began and the great point for me was to get to the rear of the fellow because I could only shoot forward with my gun. He was differently placed, for his machine gun was movable. It could fire in all directions.
> Apparently, he was no beginner, for he knew exactly that his last hour had arrived at the moment when I got at the back of

him. At that time, I had not yet the conviction 'He must fall!' which I have now on such occasions, but, on the contrary, I was curious to see whether he would fall. There is a great difference between the two feelings. When one has shot down one's first, second or third opponent, then one begins to find out how the trick is done.

My Englishman twisted and turned, going criss-cross. I did not think for a moment that the hostile squadron contained other Englishmen who conceivably might come to the aid of their comrade. I was animated by a single thought: 'The man in front of me must come down, whatever happens.' At last a favourable moment arrived. My opponent had apparently lost sight of me. Instead of twisting and turning he flew straight along. In a fraction of a second I was at his back with my excellent machine. I gave a short series of shots with my machine gun. I had gone so close that I was afraid I might dash into the Englishman.

Suddenly, I nearly yelled with joy, for the propeller of the enemy machine had stopped turning. I had shot his engine to pieces; the enemy was compelled to land, for it was impossible for him to reach his own lines. The English machine was curiously swinging to and fro. Probably something had happened to the pilot. The observer was no longer visible. His machine gun was apparently deserted. Obviously, I had hit the observer and he had fallen from his seat.

His First Victims

The Englishman landed close to the flying ground of one of our squadrons. I was so excited that I landed also and my eagerness was so great that I nearly smashed up my machine. The English flying machine and my own stood close together. I rushed to the English machine and saw that a lot of soldiers were running towards my enemy. When I arrived, I discovered that my assumption had, been correct. I had shot the engine to pieces and both the pilot and observer were severely wounded. The observer died at once and the pilot while being transported to the nearest dressing station. I honoured the fallen enemy by placing a stone on his beautiful grave.

When I came home Böelcke and my other comrades were already at breakfast. They were surprised that I had not turned up. I reported proudly that I had shot down an Englishman. All were full of joy, for I was not the only victor. As usual, Böelcke had shot down an opponent for breakfast and every one of the other men also had downed an enemy for the first time.

I would mention that since that time no English squadron ventured as far as Cambrai as long as Böelcke's squadron was there."

In his airily patronising way, Von Richthofen said:

Still, the Englishman is a smart fellow. That we must allow. Sometimes the English came down to the very low altitude and visited Böelcke in his quarters upon which they threw bombs. They absolutely challenged us to battle and never refused fighting.

Böelcke's Finish

But October 28, 1916 (when the squadron had 40 downs to its credit), Böelcke, von Richthofen and four others flying in formation saw at a distance "two impertinent Englishmen in the air who actually seemed to be enjoying the terrible weather." The struggle began. "Böelcke tackled one, I the other. I had to let go because one of the German machines got in my way." All that seems to have interested him further in the fight was the fact that Böelcke's machine suffered a sort of collision with one of the other German machines, a part of his planes was broken off, his machine was no longer steerable and it fell. Böelcke was killed.

Some little time after he had brought down his sixteenth victim von Richthofen was given the *Ordre pour le Mérite* and appointed commander of the Eleventh Chasing Squadron. It was then that the idea seized him to paint his machine a flaming red, which became afterward the personal identification of the captain, who became famous through the adventures and success he had with his machine—*Le Petit Rouge*, as "everyone got to know my red bird."

French, English, and American airmen who gained wisdom at the front may find an amusing flavour in a sage remark of von Richthofen about the time he became captain of the squadron. "In my opinion, the aggressive spirit is everything and that spirit is very strong in us Germans. Hence we shall always retain the domination of the air." Events did not altogether sustain the boast.

But it is not necessary to object strongly to the complacency of a man who fought with undiminished valour throughout his flying career, accounted for 80 enemy machines, and died at last, shot down

LIEUTENANT PAT O'BRIEN
An American youth who, in the early part of the war, joined the Canadian Royal Flying Corps. Shot down from a height of 8,000 feet, he was captured by the Germans. Afterwards making his escape, he passed through 72 days of harrowing ordeal leading finally to safety.

over the enemy's lines. If he was self-confident to the degree of vanity, his audacity was truly admirable. He lacked just ten days of attaining his twenty-sixth birthday when he fell. The English grudged him no honours.

Pat O'Brien Outwits the Hun

The Remarkable Story of an American Boy in a Seventy-Two Days' Ordeal of Escape from the Germans

The publishers of his book, *Outwitting the Hun*, were not extravagant when they advertised Lieut. Pat O'Brien's story as "one of the strangest and most thrilling since the outbreak of the war." No one else had quite such an experience, and that he lived to tell of it was due to indomitable Irish pluck rather than to any favour of circumstances. You get the flavour of the capital book he wrote and the tone of the man from the name he transferred to the title page. There is no Lieut. Patricius, or even Lieut. Patrick O'Brien; but straightforward character-delivery in plain "Lieut. Pat. O'Brien," and you get from it an odd sort of subconscious assurance that the very extraordinary story he tells of his escape from the Germans is every whit true.

Yet, between his being shot down from a height of 8,000 feet and the last item of his seventy-two days of anguish and adventure in escaping the Huns there is many a challenge to credulity. There can be but little of his story reproduced here. (His book is republished by Leonaur in *War with the R. F. C.: Two Personal Accounts of Airmen During the First World War, 1914-18* along with *A Soldier of the Sky* by George F. Campbell.)

As a Fighting Scout

Pat started flying, in Chicago, in 1912, he says:

> I was then eighteen years old," "but I had had a hankering for the air ever since I can remember....
> In the early part of 1916, when trouble was brewing in Mexico, I joined the American Flying Corps. I was sent to San Diego, where the army flying school is located, and spent about eight months there, but as I was anxious to get into active service and there didn't seem much chance of America ever getting into the war, I resigned and, crossing over to Canada, joined the Royal Flying Corps at Victoria, B. C.
> I was sent to Camp Borden, Toronto, first to receive instruction

and later to instruct. While a cadet I made the first loop ever made by a cadet in Canada, and after I had performed the stunt I half expected to be kicked out of the service for it. Apparently, however, they considered the source and let it go at that. Later on, I had the satisfaction of introducing the loop as part of the regular course of instruction for cadets in the R. F. C, and I want to say right here that Camp Borden has turned out some of the best fliers that have ever gone to France.

In May, 1917, I and seventeen other Canadian fliers left for England on the *Megantic*, where we were to qualify for service in France. . . .

Within a few weeks after our arrival in England all of us had won our 'wings'—the insignia worn on the left breast by every pilot on the western front.

We were all sent to a place in France known as the Pool Pilots' Mess. Here men gather from all the training squadrons in Canada and England and await assignments to the particular squadron of which they are to become members.

He was soon "called" to a squadron stationed about eighteen miles back of the Ypres Line. There were eighteen pilots. The routine was two flights a day, each of two hours' duration. He presently found that his squadron "was some hot squadron," the fliers being assigned to special-duty work, "such as shooting up trenches at a height of fifty feet from the ground."

Captured by the Hun

Pat holds August 17, 1917, as a day he will "not easily forget." He has fairly good reason for thinking the day a fixity in his memory, for, as he says:

I killed two Huns in a double-seated machine in the morning, another in the evening, and then I was captured myself. I may have spent more eventful days in my life, but I can't recall any just now.

Considering the fact that he had been shot down from a height of 8,000 feet the miracle is that he became "a prisoner of war." His fellows of the squadron who had seen the fight took it as a matter of fact that he had been killed outright. One realises that a chap who could come through that sort of juggle with death was quite equal to his later adventures.

Convalescent, after some time spent in a hospital, O'Brien was sent to the officers' prison camp at Courtrai, preparatory to transfer to a prison in the interior of Germany. He remained there nearly three weeks, to which he devotes an interesting chapter. He had many fellow prisoners, and, of course, one frequent topic of conversation was "what were the chances of escape?"

There were many ingenious plans but O'Brien did not remain to attempt to carry out any of them. September 9th, he and six other officers were marked off for transfer into Germany, and later were marched to the train that was to convey them. They were objects of derision to the crowd gathered at the station. There were twelve coaches, eleven of them containing troops going home on leave, the twelfth, fourth class, filthy, being reserved for the prisoners, eight of them under four guards.

He proposed to the other officers that if the eight of them would at a given signal jump on the four guards and overpower them, they could, when the train slowed down on approaching a village, leap to the ground and take to flight. But the others turned the plan down on the ground that if they did get free they would be recaptured speedily. O'Brien therefore resolved to make a try on his own account by a leap from a window when the train was in motion. After long self-debate, as they were getting nearer and nearer to their destination he successfully put his resolution into effect.

Making His Escape

Then began one of the most remarkable series of perils, hardships, struggles and curious adventures that fell to the lot of any individual in the course of the war. With the aid of a map, which he had stolen from a guard's room at Courtrai, he set out with the distant Holland frontier as his objective. It is a narrative that loses by condensation, for there is hardly an adventure or experience that has not novel interest as O'Brien relates it. To avoid detection and capture he had to secrete himself by day, all his travel being by night. His guide was the Pole Star. "But for it I wouldn't be here today."

About the ninth night he crossed into Luxemburg, but though the principality was officially neutral it offered no safer haven than Belgium would. Discovery would have been followed by the same consequences as capture in Germany proper. In the nine nights, he had travelled perhaps seventy-five miles.

He was nine or ten days getting across Luxemburg, a task that could have been accomplished in two days of normal travel, but swollen feet and knees, aching body and a hunger-griping stomach together with the necessity of stealth to avoid discovery, German guards, workmen and others often having to be widely circled, are not conducive to speed. About the eighteenth day after his leap from the train he entered Belgium, and some days later brought up at the Meuse between Namur and Huy, where it was at least half a mile wide. There he came nearest of all to giving up the struggle. But he must get across. There was nothing to do but swim.

There were adventures in Belgium, some amusing, some harrowing, all of them perilous to an English officer escaped from captivity. When, after narrow escapes not a few he reached the Holland frontier, one of the greatest of his herculean tasks presented itself. He had to pass the triple barbed-wire barrier with its electrically charged nine-foo-thigh fence. With hands and sticks he resolutely set to work to dig under the deadly barrier—hard work and most dangerous. He was forced to stop from time to time to escape detection. At last, on November 19, 1917, the hole was finished. He writhed through and into Holland territory.

A few more difficulties to surmount, then on board train for Rotterdam, a run to London, a presentation to the king, some banquet pleasures in London and, crowning all, home again, "in the little town of Momence, Illinois, on the Kankakee River."

A Track and Trackless Winner

Eddie Rickenbacker, Who Won Popularity as an Auto Racer, Snatched Lasting Glory from the Void.

The spirit of adventure had won for Eddie Rickenbacker a wide popularity long before he began plucking laurels from the skies. His performances as an automobile racer had made him the idol of lovers of that perilous sport and taught him the cool judgment and generalship in dealing with velocities which served him to such good purpose when he exchanged automobiles for aeroplanes. When America entered the war, Rickenbacker was in England on automobile business, but hastened back to America with the intention of organizing a flying squadron of motor drivers for service in France. His plan was not possible at the time from the government point of view, and Rickenbacker accepted the position of chauffeur to General Pershing and sailed with that officer.

It was not long after, however, that the loftier ambition found its channel and at Villeneuve, March 4, 1918, he became a member of Squadron 94, the so-called "Hat-in-the-Ring" squadron of which Major Lufbery was the commander. Lufbery was then America's top ace, his service of more than three years in the French Air Service and with the Lafayette Escadrille having netted him seventeen Huns, omitting those not officially recorded. A little over two months later, May 19, 1918, Major Lufbery was killed by a leap from his flaming machine.

The title of American Ace of Aces passed from Lufbery to Lieutenant Paul Baer, who, with a record of nine victories, had not gotten over his repugnance to shooting down an enemy aviator. Two days later Baer was shot down and captured. Lieutenant Frank Bayliss succeeded to the title. He was killed June 12th with 13 victories to his credit. Then David Putnam, with 12 victories, took the lead. He was shot down in flames. Rickenbacker, who in the period between March and July had accounted for seven enemy machines, next was ace of aces for a brief time, but Frank Luke took the title from him in a single day's stunning exploit, as told in the special story of that amazing young man.

In due course, however, the Rickenbacker record grew becomingly and in addition to attaining the highest score on downs he conspicuously distinguished himself in the service as Squadron Commander. Some of his eulogists do not hesitate to give him pre-eminence as a commander because of the judgment he exercised in protecting himself and guarding the safety of less competent pilots.

Not a few aviators have written books descriptive of their experiences and there is quite a library of these high adventure stories; but it is probable that the uncommonly voluminous book Rickenbacker has contributed to the long list is one of the most valuable because of the great variety of interesting matter it comprises. Indeed, *Fighting the Flying Circus* has historic importance as well as storied interest and is not by any means a glorification of its author.

That fact makes it rather difficult to take from the book the material wanted for a personal sketch without including attractive matter that would speedily exceed our limits of space—for example, the complete narrative of the exploit with "Rumpler Number 16"; or the story of Douglas Campbell, America's first ace; or the story of Jimmy Meissner, who piloted his machine with the canvas gone; and others.

Chagrin a Saving Grace

Before Rickenbacker scored a victory, he suffered many disap-

CAPTAIN "EDDIE" RICKENBACKER WITH HIS MOTHER AND SISTER

pointments, and felt the chagrin of seeing his expected quarry escape. There was serviceable virtue in it all nevertheless, as he admits in his account of downing his first Hun. He says:

> My preparation for combat fighting in the air was a gradual one. As I look back upon it now, it seems that I had the rare good fortune to experience almost every variety of danger that can beset the war pilot before I ever fired a shot at an enemy from an aeroplane.
> This good fortune is rare, it appears to me. Many a better man than myself has leaped into his stride and begun accumulating victories from his very first flight over the lines. It was a brilliant start for him and his successes brought him instant renown. But he had been living on the cream at the start and was unused to the skim-milk of aviation. One day the cream gave out and the first dose of skim-milk terminated his career.
> So, despite the weeks and weeks of disappointment that attended my early fighting career, I appreciated even then the enormous benefit that I would reap later from these experiences. I can now most solemnly affirm that had I won my first victory during my first trips over the lines I believe I would never have survived a dozen combats. Every disappointment that came to me brought with it an enduring lesson that repaid me eventually tenfold. If any one of my antagonists had been through the same school of disappointments that had so annoyed me it is probable that he, instead of me, would now be telling his friends back home about his series of victories over the enemy.

It was April 29, 1918, that he had his turn of luck. He was in the air with Captain James Norman Hall following a course towards Pont-à-Mousson, as that experienced flyer led the way.

> Whether or not he knew all along that a German craft was in that region I could not tell. But when he began to change his direction and curve up into the sun I followed close behind him knowing that there was a good reason for this manoeuvre. I looked earnestly about me in every direction.
> Yes! There was a scout coming towards us from north of Pont-à-Mousson. It was at about our altitude. I knew it was a Hun the moment I saw it, for it had the familiar lines of their new *Pfalz*. Moreover, my confidence in James Norman Hall was such that I knew he couldn't make a mistake. And he was still

climbing into the sun, carefully keeping his position between its glare and the oncoming fighting plane. I clung as closely to Hall as I could. The Hun was steadily approaching us, unconscious of his danger, for we were full in the sun.

With the first downward dive of Jimmy's machine I was by his side. We had at least a thousand feet advantage over the enemy and we were two to one numerically. He might outdive our machines, for the *Pfalz* is a famous diver, while our faster climbing Nieuports had a droll little habit of shedding their fabric when plunged too furiously through the air. The Boche hadn't a chance to outfly us. His only salvation would be in a dive towards his own lines.

These thoughts passed through my mind in a flash and I instantly determined upon my tactics. While Hall went in for his attack I would keep my altitude and get a position the other side of the *Pfalz*, to cut off his retreat.

No sooner had I altered my line of flight than the German pilot saw me leave the sun's rays. Hall was already halfway to him when he stuck up his nose and began furiously climbing to the upper ceiling. I let him pass me and found myself on the other side just as Hall began firing. I doubt if the Boche had seen Hall's Nieuport at all.

Surprised by discovering this new antagonist, Hall, ahead of him, the *Pfalz* immediately abandoned all idea of a battle and banking around to the right started for home, just as I had expected him to do. In a trice, I was on his tail. Down, down we sped with throttles both full open. Hall was coming on somewhere in my rear. The Boche had no heart for evolutions or manoeuvres. He was running like a scared rabbit, as I had run from Campbell. I was gaining upon him every instant and had my sights trained dead upon his seat before I fired my first shot.

Without a Return Shot

"At 150 yards, I pressed my triggers. The tracer bullets cut a streak of living fire into the rear of the Pfalz tail. Raising the nose of my aeroplane slightly the fiery streak lifted itself like a stream of water pouring from a garden hose. Gradually it settled into the pilot's seat. The swerving of the *Pfalz* course indicated that its rudder no longer was held by a directing hand. At 2,000 feet above the enemy's lines I pulled up my headlong dive and

CAPTAIN JAMES NORMAN HALL
An American ace who was captured,
and made a prisoner of war by the Germans.

watched the enemy machine continuing on its course. Curving slightly to the left the *Pfalz* circled a little to the south and the next minute crashed onto the ground just at the edge of the woods a mile inside their own lines. I had brought down my first enemy aeroplane and had not been subjected to a single shot!"

So capital a beginning had an appropriate sequence of performances and honours to match, among them, as early as May 15th, the *Croix de Guerre*. That day, too, Lieutenant Jimmy Meissner, the merriest, most reckless member of the squadron, took to his breast the *Croix de Guerre*, and much ado the two had to keep their elation within the limits of decorum, which stunt flying for the entertainment of the French officials did not diminish. Rickenbacker says:

> Suddenly Jimmy Meissner stood by my side, grinning his most winsome grin. 'Rick,' said he, 'I feel that "Hate-the-Hun" feeling creeping over me. What do you say to going up and getting a Boche?'
> 'Right!' I called back over my shoulder. 'Come along. We'll take a real ride.'
> As luck would have it, we had hardly left the ground when we saw a Hun two-seater, probably a *Rumpler* machine, very high above us. The *Rumpler* has the highest ceiling of any of the German two-seaters and frequently they sail along above us at an elevation quite impossible for the Nieuport to reach. It is maddening to attain one's maximum height and see the enemy still sailing imperturbably along, taking his photographs and scorning even to fire an occasional burst at one.
> We climbed at our fastest to overtake this fellow before he could reach his safety spot. Evidently, he got 'wind up' for after a few minutes climbing he sheered off towards Germany and disappeared from our view. We completed our patrol of the lines without finding another enemy in the sky and returned to our field, where we landed with the mutual vow that on the morrow we would begin seriously our palm collecting shows until we might dangle our new *Croix de Guerre* well down below our knees.
> Jimmy looked contemplatively down at my long legs.
> 'Have a heart, Rick!' he said softly, 'think of the cost of the red tape!'

MAJOR JAMES A. MEISSNER
He was decorated for bravery in action in the Toul
sector. He attacked many enemy observation balloons.
He was shot down in his plane several times.

As combats in the air, however varied in the performance, have a great similarity in narrative, it were bootless to follow the captain through the many experiences that earned his distinction. The earlier incidents were when the squadron was confined to the use of Nieuports because more satisfactory machines were not available. He dwells with some pride of possession on the later equipment of Spads. Soon after getting them he had become Flight Commander, and relates an unusual experience to illustrate the extent to which the Flight Leader of a squadron feels himself morally bound to go.

> Six of my Spads were following me in a morning's patrol over the enemy's lines in the vicinity of Rheims. We were well along towards the front when we discovered a number of aeroplanes far above us and somewhat behind our side of the lines. While we made a circle or two, all the while steadily climbing for higher altitude, we observed the darting machines above us exchanging shots at one another. Suddenly the fracas developed into a regular free-for-all.
> Reaching a slightly higher altitude at a distance of a mile or two to the east of the *mêlée*, I collected my formation and headed about for the attack. Just then I noticed that one side had evidently been victorious. Seven aeroplanes remained together in compact formation. The others had streaked it away, each man for himself.

Seven to Seven

> As we drew nearer we saw that the seven conquerors were in fact enemy machines. There was no doubt about it. They were *Fokkers*. Their opponents, whether American, French or British, had been scattered and had fled. The *Fokkers* had undoubtedly seen our approach and had very wisely decided to keep their formation together rather than separate to pursue their former antagonists. They were climbing to keep my squad ever a little below them, while they decided upon their next move.
> We were seven and they were seven. It was a lovely morning with clear visibility, and all my pilots, I knew, were keen for a fight. I looked over the skies and discovered no reason why we shouldn't take them on at any terms they might require. Accordingly, I set our course a little steeper and continued straight on towards them.
> The Spad is a better climber than the *Fokker*. Evidently the Bo-

che pilots opposite us knew this fact. Suddenly the last four in their formation left their line of flight and began to draw away in the direction of Soissons—still climbing. The three *Fokkers* in front continued towards us for another minute or two. When we were separated by less than a quarter of a mile the three *Heinies* decided that they had done enough for their country, and putting down their noses, they began a steep dive for their lines.

To follow them was so obvious a thing to do that I began at once to speculate upon what this manoeuvre meant to them. The four rear *Fokkers* were well away by now, but the moment we began to dive after the three ahead of us they would doubtless be prompt to turn and select a choice position behind our tails. Very well! We would bank upon this expectation of theirs and make our plans accordingly!

We were at about 17,000 feet altitude. The lines were almost directly under us. Following the three retreating *Fokkers* at our original level, we soon saw them disappear well back into Germany. Now for the wily four that were probably still climbing for altitude!

Arriving over Fismes I altered our course and pointed it towards Soissons, and as we flew we gained an additional thousand feet. Exactly upon the scheduled time we perceived approaching us the four *Fokkers* who were now satisfied that they had us at a disadvantage and might either attack or escape, as they desired. They were, however, at precisely the same altitude at which we were now flying.

Wigwagging my wings as a signal for the attack, I sheered slightly to the north of them to cut off their retreat. They either did not see my manoeuvre or else they thought we were friendly aeroplanes, for they came on dead ahead like a flock of silly geese. At two hundred yards, I began firing.

Not until we were within fifty yards of each other did the Huns show any signs of breaking. I had singled out the flight leader and had him nicely within my sights, when he suddenly piqued downwards, the rest of his formation immediately following him. At the same instant one of my guns—the one having a double feed—hopelessly jammed. And after a burst of twenty shots or so from the other gun it likewise failed me! There was no time to pull away for repairs!

Both my guns were useless. For an instant, I considered the advisability of withdrawing while I tried to free the jam. But the opportunity was too good to lose. The pilots behind me would be thrown into some confusion when I signalled them to carry on without me. And moreover, the enemy pilots would quickly discover my trouble and would realize that the flight leader was out of the fight. I made up my mind to go through with the fracas without guns and trust to luck to see the finish. The next instant we were ahead of the quartet and were engaged in a furious dog-fight.

Every man was for himself. The Huns were excellent pilots and seemed to be experienced fighters. Time and again I darted into a good position behind or below a tempting target, with the sole result of compelling the Fritz to alter his course and get out of his position of supposed danger. If he had known I was unarmed he would have had me at his mercy. As it was I would no sooner get into a favourable position behind him than he would double about and the next moment I found myself compelled to look sharp to my own safety.

In this manner, the whole revolving circus went tumbling across the heavens—always dropping lower and steadily traveling deeper into the German lines. Two of my pilots had abandoned the scrap and turned homewards. Engines or guns had failed them. When at last we had fought down to 3,000 feet and were some four miles behind their lines, I observed two flights of enemy machines coming up from the rear to their rescue. We had none of us secured a single victory—but neither had the Huns. Personally, I began to feel a great longing for home. I dashed out ahead of the foremost Spad and frantically wigwagging him to attention I turned my little 'bus towards our lines. With a feeling of great relief, I saw that all four were following me and that the enemy reinforcements were not in any position to dispute our progress.

On the way, homeward I struggled with my jammed guns—but to no result. Despite every precaution these weapons will fail a pilot when most needed. I had gone through with a nerve-racking scrap, piquing upon deadly opponents with a harmless machine. My whole safety had depended upon their not knowing it.

As Squadron Commander

The night of September 24th Rickenbacker received the order promoting him to the command of the 94 Squadron, his pride and pleasure being greater than he could find words to express. He had been with the squadron since the first day at the front; but three of the original members were left—Reed Chambers, Thorn Taylor, and himself. He took counsel for himself that night and formulated rules for himself. He would never ask a pilot to go on a mission he would not undertake himself. He would lead by example as well as by precept. He would accompany the new pilots to watch their errors and give them more confidence by showing their dangers. He would work harder than ever he did as a pilot.

Full of enthusiasm to carry out his purpose he started out the next morning on a lone, voluntary patrol and within half an hour returned to the aerodrome with two more victories to his credit—"the first double-header I had so far won." He discovered a pair of L.V.G. two-seater machines, above which was a formation of five *Fokkers*. From a position, well up in the sun Rickenbacker drove down at the nearest *Fokker* and sent it crashing with the first volley. The Huns were so surprised by the suddenness of the attack and the drop of one of them that their only thought was of escape. Before they recovered their wits and renewed their formation, one of the L.V.G. two-seaters was shot down in flames, and quite content with his morning's work Rickenbacker put on gas and piqued for home.

October 30th Rickenbacker won his 25th and 26th victories, the last that were added to his score. But on November 9th Major Kirby, who had just joined the 94 Squadron for a little air fighting experience, was one of a party of four who flew off for a try at the retreating Huns, and shot down an enemy plane across the Meuse. This was the last plane shot down in the war. Rather exultingly, pardonably so, Captain Rickenbacker says:

> Our old 94 Squadron had won the first American victory over enemy aeroplanes when Alan Winslow and Douglas Campbell had dropped two biplane machines, on the Toul aerodrome. 94 Squadron had been first to fly over the lines and had completed more hours flying at the front than any other American organization. It had won more victories than any other—and now, for the last word, it had the credit of bringing down the last enemy aeroplane of the war!

And this word from Laurence Driggs:

> After having visited some sixty-odd British flying squadrons at the front, many of the French *escadrilles* and all of the American squadrons, I was given the pleasure of entering Germany, after the armistice was signed, as the guest of the Hat-in-the-Ring Squadron, of which Captain Rickenbacker was and is the commanding officer. In no other organisation in France did I find so great a loyalty to a leader, such true squadron fraternal ism, such subordination of the individual to the organisation. In other words, the commander of 94 Squadron had perfected the finest flying corps I have ever seen.

An Aviator's Story of Bombarding the Enemy
Told by a French Aviator

This is a tale of the risks, the courage, the fears, the luck, the compulsion of duty and the haunting memory of destruction that mark the fighting service of the airmen. It is a French aviator's plain tale of experience from Illustration, Paris.

1—Our Flight at Daybreak

When our flight commander came in we knew by his smiling face that he had something interesting for us.

"Make a careful inspection," he said. "The staff counts on you to destroy a station of great importance. Take oil and essence enough for four hours' flight. Each of you will carry five 90's and one 155. If you do not wholly destroy the place during the first attack, rest, go back tomorrow and finish your work. You will get explicit orders before you start."

Our service is not confined to the defence of Paris. We are not the G. V. C. of the skies. We had no idea where we were going; but our chief was in such good spirits that we looked for a fine adventure. So full of ardour, we all, pilots and engineers, inspected our great flyers. Then, in view of resting for our work, we turned in for the night. When someone knocked violently on my door I sprang up broad awake.

"Get up, sergeant!" cried a voice. "It is nearly three o'clock! You will be late!"

The motors were turning on the ground. I dressed hastily and went out.... Brr! it was cold. The field lay like a shadow in the moonlight; the sky was of ideal clearness; a light fog was rising from the damp ground. Our whole assembly, pilots and observers, went into the little shack used as our flight bureau. Then came a great hand-clasping, farewells—silence.

The commander pointed out our route and we traced it on our charts. Now we knew where we were going and what we had to do.

There were our machines in the half-light, drawn up in line of battle. Every pilot cast a swift glance at his craft as he went aboard. They tested the motors. The grinding of the motors had slowed down; there was an instant of relative calm. An order passed from pilot to pilot: "Start from right to left, thirty seconds headway!"

A long rattle broke the silence; an *avion* glided over the ground and went up: *Our Chief!* I was second. I heard my friends wishing me luck. I rolled on at full speed, rose, and rushed out, into the darkness.

When I had been flying ten minutes I realised that something was the matter. My motor was not "giving." The altimeter marked 1,800 meters. I saw the trenches stretching like cobwebs across the ground. I tried to rise—*Impossible!* I was less than 2,000 meters above the earth; I was under orders; it was up to me to get to my destination and destroy the object I had been sent to destroy; and my motor would not raise me one foot. For one moment, sickly doubt assailed me. I crossed the line and, instantly, my craft was a target. The explosion of the bombs was so violent and the bombs were so near, and there was so many of them, that the air was in a tumult. My machine oscillated. The noise was head-splitting; the muzzles of their 77's formed a bar of fire. I was taking heavy risks, but what else could I do? *I must get there and do my work.*

The 105 was going; so were the 77's, upward like a bit of fireworks, hurrying along towards the zenith until his lamps were like little stars. On the following day we set out again to do our work. *We had been sent to destroy.*

2—We Dropped Bombs on the Enemy

We started at four o'clock in the afternoon and landed to reconnoitre at a camp near the lines. While the motormen examined our motors, and while the electricians put in the lights, we automobiled to a nearby town and ate our dinner. We were dressed for our trip. The time set for our ascension was nine o'clock.

At dinner, the chief had said to us: "When my lights go out you will know that I am flying as a bird flies *for their lines!*" As we stood there watching his flight his lights went out. That was his signal to us;

his farewell. But we saw him once more when his swift black plane cut across the disk of the yellow moon.

Then I went up. I rose to a height of 600 meters. I turned my last spiral and put out my lights and the lights fixed to the wings, leaving nothing but the little chart lamp.

The earth lay away below us, vast, dark and still. We heard no sound, we saw no light save the pallid light of the moon. The wind was strong. I had no guiding points. I steered by the stars. As we approached the lines the broad fan of a searchlight fixed upon me. I made a rapid turn. Something was coming. We saw two light-bombs and three golden *fusees* shooting worms of fire.

After a flight of fifty minutes we reached our objective point. I slowed down and we descended. When 500 meters above the earth we dropped incendiary cans and bombs. A shower of light bombs answered us; they showed us what we were doing and made it easier to do our work. Then the lights of powerful projectors fastened on us. But our work was done, and before long we were over our landing.

The home run before the light wind was a pleasure. *But a man always remembers*, and the thought of the damage I had done haunted me! They fired their cannon. We were so close to them I wondered they did not hit us. On that occasion, my big machine did well because my motors were normal. But, to sum it all up in a few words, everything was in my favour this last time. We escaped, and, what is more important, we contributed not a little to the success of the French in Champagne.

A Bombing Expedition with the British Air Service

DARING ADVENTURES OF THE ROYAL FLIERS

Told by First Lieutenant J. Errol D. Boyd, of the British Air Service

The feats of the British fliers form a thrilling chapter of modern heroism. Their exploits are innumerable. In the defence of London from Zeppelin raids, on the Western and Eastern battlefront, in the Dardanelles, over the deserts of Africa, and along the valleys of the Nile—they are not unlike the crusaders of old in their heroism. We here present one typical narrative—it is the story of a Canadian, from Toronto, who relates his own thrilling experience to a war correspondent of the *New York World* at The Hague.

"Boydie," as his friends call him, was shot down by a German anti-aircraft gun from the almost unbelievable height of 12,000 feet. Three cylinders were torn away from his engine. The wings were pierced in five places. His machine dropped two miles, twisting and turning, looping the loop ten times on his way down. It finally landed, right-side up, with the young Canadian safe and sound, just fifty yards inside of Dutch territory. He sprang from his seat and gave brisk battle to the soldiers of Queen Wilhelmina. They overpowered him, and interned him, but not until there'd been a considerable mix-up, in which fists and noses figured prominently—Boydie's fists and some Dutch noses.

1—"BOYDIE'S" OWN STORY OF ADVENTURE

It's the greatest game, the greatest thrill in the world! I used to think that driving a motorcar 100 miles an hour was fun. I was in that game in Canada for a while. Then I thought that just riding in a slow old biplane 'bus was a pretty keen proposition. But a chap never knows what real sport is until he's driving his own fast machine, with a pal working a machine gun, and going after the other fellow hell-bent for election. That's the life!

It makes me laugh now to think of the old biplane "pushers"—with the propellers at the rear—that I used to fool with. Old Farnams and Curtises and Wrights. Why, a chap was lucky to get 65 or 70 miles an hour out of some of them.

It was the proudest day of my life when they gave me my flying ticket and a speedy little Nieuport biplane and said: "Here she is, Boydie. Take her over the Channel. Beat it for Dunkirk. Some of the others are going across this afternoon, so you won't get lost if you follow them. Top o' the luck to you, old Toronto." Half a dozen other machines went sailing over the water, 5,000 feet high, that spring morning doing a leisurely eighty miles an hour and spaced as evenly as a squadron of battleships in parade formation. The leaders were circling about and descending toward an immense open space in front of a long row of hangars at Dunkirk.

It wasn't long after that before I got into my first scrap. I never will forget that, for I made a bally fool out of myself and was mighty glad to get back alive to the station. I had a pretty good machine, a Moran monoplane equipped with a machine gun, and an old chap called Gott, a sergeant, went up with me and sat in the gun seat. I was wild to see the German lines.

"Go and take a look at them," the C. O. said, "but don't cross or you'll probably get jolly well peppered. Those 'Archies' (anti-aircraft guns) can shoot pretty far and pretty straight, you know."

2—We Fight 8,000 Feet in Air

I promised to be careful and up we went. At about 8,000 feet I headed her for the German trenches, and in a few minutes, we were right over them. Old Gott gave me a nudge then, and right ahead of us, a few miles off, I saw two German Albatross machines coming right for us. Old Gott and I had our telephones on and he said: "What about it. Lieutenant?"

"What do you say if we let 'em have a bit?" I asked him.

"Right-o, sir," said Gott. He was a game chap, that old fellow, and he'd been in many a scrap. I often wonder whether he's still all right. Well, he had a belt of cartridges on the gun, and he got ready to spin 'em out. I stuck the nose of the old bus up in the air and tried to get on top of the Germans. My machine was a better climber than theirs, and so when we passed I was a couple of hundred feet higher. Old

Gott pointed the gun at 'em and kept working the trigger. I could see the flames shooting out of the muzzle. But the Boches were pretty busy too. I caught sight of their gunmen working away with their quick-firers as we passed. With the rush of air it was impossible to feel the whiz of any of their bullets; but I knew jolly well that they were pretty close to us, and we found later a lot of holes in our wings.

Well, all of us wheeled, and at it we went again. Gott put on another belt of cartridges and let 'em have it. As we passed the second time one of the Albatrosses dropped a couple of hundred feet. I thought that Gott had winged the pilot, but it must have been only an airhole they struck, for they straightened out and went on.

They're speedy beggars, those Albatrosses. By the time I got turned again and straightened out they were half a mile or so off and driving like the devil over their own country—running away from us.

"Let's go after them and give 'em what-for, Gott!" I said.

"Very good, sir," he answered.

So, after them we went. I gave the old bus all she had, but I couldn't overtake the Albatrosses, nor even get near enough to have another shot at them. Mile after mile we drove until, finally, we came to a town—Ghent it must have been—and I thought it was about time to start back. We were only about 6,000 feet high.

All of a sudden there was a little white cloud directly in front of us, a few hundred yards off. We plunged right through it, and I got a sniff of some strong acid-like odour. Then little white clouds began to appear at our sides, and below us and above us. Gott pointed upward and I made the machine climb as hard as she could without standing right on our tail.

I realised then that the Albatrosses had purposely run away from us to lead us into a trap. They had led us right over a long line of "Archies."

There we were, twenty miles or so from home, with every anti-aircraft gun the Germans had peppering away at us. We certainly made a race for it. There was no use circling around and climbing. The only thing to do was to go up as best we could while driving, straight ahead, and trust to luck. To get home was the one thing we wanted.

It took us perhaps fourteen or fifteen minutes to do the twenty-odd miles. And in every mile of that distance there were at least two or three Archies letting drive at us. A couple of minor wires were struck, and old Gott had his clothes torn by a bit of shell. I didn't get hit. But it sure was a hot dash for home, and we were a couple of lucky chaps to get there. I got an awful ragging from the C. O. for being such a fool. Never again did I drive over the German territory so close to the earth as 8,000 feet!

3—My Bombing Expedition

I did week after week of scout work, driving over Belgium with observers who noted the movement of German troops from place to place, or took photographs of the trenches and the fortifications back of them, or plotted out the exact location of supply stations and the like, for the purpose of bombing them later.

That's a snappy sport—bombing—but you've got to watch your step, as you say in the States. You mustn't forget to let go all of your bombs before you come down, or you'll be smashed up yourself. I knew one poor chap who made a landing with two bombs he'd forgotten to drop. That was the end of him and his machine. There wasn't much left of either.

It was on a bombing expedition that I met my big adventure—the one that landed me in this country, technically a prisoner.

It was on Oct. 3. Three of us set out with orders to let go a few T-N-T's on some hangars and supply sheds the Germans had at Zeebrugge, some forty odd miles up the coast from our station at Dunkirk. Each of us had six 75-pound bombs under the body of our machine. Pretty deadly things those 75-pounders. They'll make quite a smash. Then I had a dozen or more little hand-bombs, five or six pounders. They're nasty beggars, too. You don't want to be too close to the spot where they land.

We got away in the dark, about 4 o'clock, and, back of our own lines, climbed till we were about 10,000 feet up. Then we headed up the coast and got over the town of Zeebrugge just as daylight was appearing. We located the sheds we wanted, and one after the other of us let go at them. It's a great thing to pull your lever, let the old bomb go whizzing down for nearly two miles, and then wheel around and wait to see what she'll do when she hits. Of course, you can't hear anything, but you see a puff, a burst of earth, and, if you're lucky, maybe you'll see a building go to smash.

Well, it didn't take long for them to know that we were over them, and they began to let drive with their Archies. The shells began to burst pretty close to my old R. E. P.—a fast, single-passenger monoplane I was driving that day—but I stuck around and let drop all six T-N-T's and hand-bombs. I was separated from the other chaps by this time, and didn't see them, in fact.

I heard in a roundabout way afterward that one of my bombs killed fourteen men and four horses. I don't know whether that's true or not. The story had it that several of the men killed were Belgians. I hope that part of it's wrong. But that's the luck of the game.

Pretty soon a bomb bullet burst only a couple of hundred feet away from me, and right on my level, although my gauge showed me that I was pretty close to 11,000 feet. I said to myself: "You'd best stick her nose up, Boydie, or they'll get you. These Archies must be new ones, for they're throwing steel higher than any I ever saw before."

So, I climbed and climbed, circling around, until I was a few hundred feet over 12,000. There I felt absolutely safe, and began to look around to see where I was. I had passed completely over Zeebrugge and was pretty well up the coast toward a sort of a strait. I thought I'd best turn around and make back for home while the making was good. So, I wheeled and began to think about breakfast. The only thing in my mind at the moment was that I was hungry.

The next thing I knew there was a blinding smash right in front of me. I realized two things—that my propeller was gone and that I was falling like a stone. They'd got me at last. I didn't know whether I'd been hit anywhere or not. I just gave everything up and began to see pretty little pictures of Toronto and New York and my girl in Cleveland, and all that sort of thing. Believe me, I was a scared Canadian. It looked like curtains for J. Errol Dunston Boyd.

But—you know how it is: if a fellow falls into the water he tries to swim anyhow, even if he can't. He does something instinctively to help himself. So, I kept on trying, working my levers without half knowing what I was doing.

You've seen that "falling leaf" stunt that the trick fliers do, haven't you—where the machine just flops from side to side as it comes down, swinging this way and then the other way? Well, that's what my old R. E. P. was doing. Then she'd loop. Some chaps who saw me coming down said she looped nine or ten times. I'd looped before, but never involuntarily. I was strapped in of course, or I'd have beaten the old bus down to the ground.

4—I Dropped 12,000 Feet from Clouds

I don't know how long it takes to drop 12,000 feet. The scientists can figure it out. But, believe me, it doesn't take very long. I was in a sort of a daze from the time I was struck, but it seemed only a couple of seconds before I saw the ground right under me, and—I couldn't believe it then—I was right side up and on a decent angle for landing. I lifted her nose a little bit just before striking, and, so help me, Bob, I got her on the ground with scarcely a bump.

About a quarter of a mile off were a lot of soldiers in grey uniforms. They began to run toward me. "Well, I'll give you German beggars a little row before you stick me in one of your filthy prison camps," I said to myself. As soon as I got the old bus to a standstill I unstrapped myself and jumped out. When the grey-backs got within a hundred yards of me I let drive at them with my service revolver. I slammed all seven shots at 'em, but missed.

I must have been a bit balmy in the bean, for I didn't notice that they weren't firing at me. Then I did a nutty stunt. You know we carry "light pistols." They're things that you use to shoot coloured balls of fire with at night, for signalling purposes, when you're going to land, and all that. It happened that I grabbed my light pistol as I jumped out of the seat, so I thought, "I'll give you this, too, you dirty Boches!" And I shot half a dozen beautiful balls of fire at them. I was raging mad.

Then they surrounded me. I'm pretty husky, you see. I've got 180 pounds, and at that time I was hard as nails; so, a couple of them, you can bet, took some good wallops before a dozen or so piled on top of me and pinned me down. They began shouting things at me in some language that I didn't understand.

Finally, one of them said in English: "We're not your enemies. We're not Germans. This is Holland and we're Dutchmen."

Only then did I stop scrapping with them. They let me up and stood around me with their bayonets ready to give me a jab in case I started anything more. It was some little time before I was able to stop puffing and give a look around at the scenery. Only fifty yards away was the border line between Belgium and Holland, marked by a heavy barbed-wired entanglement and two or three cables through which ran high powered electric currents.

On the other side of the fence were a hundred or more Boches—patrols who had hoped to capture me if I alighted on their side of the barbed wire. But I just beat them to it by a few measly feet. A close shave, what? And weren't they sore. They yelled over the fence at me, and shook their fists and guns; but I swore back at them just as hard as they cussed me.

The Dutch were pretty good to me when I quieted down. They were decent fellows and were only doing their duty in grabbing me for internment. They took me up to a fort in Groningen, and there I stuck from Oct. 3 until the first of this year, when I was instructed by the British Government to give my parole. That meant that I must promise on my word of honour as an officer and gentleman not to try to escape.

I could have got away, I think. I had all arrangements made to make a dash from the fort one dark night, have an automobile waiting outside to rush me to the coast, and I even had a trawler ready to take me and some other chaps back to England. But before we were quite ready to make our dash the word came to give our parole, and we had to abandon the plan.

Lost on a Seaplane and Set Adrift in a Mine-Field

Adventures on the North Sea
Told by a Seaplane Observer

The Great War has introduced new perils both on land and sea. Here is the story of one of them—two men drifting through a mine-field on a crippled seaplane, fending off mines with their bare hands, and expecting every moment to be blown to pieces! Daring adventure told in the Wide World.

1—My Hundredth Flight Over the North Sea

I completed my "century" of seaplane flights over the North Sea with an adventure the like of which, I trust, will never occur again.

Many varied experiences have gone to total up that number of ascents—some far from pleasant, others most interesting, and well repaying one for occasional hardships.

The sequel to my one-hundredth flight, however, will take a lot of effacing from my memory.

The atmosphere was a trifle thick when we started off from our base with the intention of flying an ordinary hundred-and-fifty-mile circular patrol.

The farther we progressed, the thicker grew the haze, till we at last were travelling through dense fog.

We left at 7.30 a.m., and climbed to two thousand five hundred feet to get above the heat-haze and fog over the water.

At eight-twenty-five, almost an hour later, the revolutions of the eight-foot tractor began slackening perceptibly, and presently, to our dismay, the engine stopped dead.

We were compelled to descend so quickly that there was no time to send a wireless signal; in fact, I just barely managed to cut the trailing aerial wire free before we struck the sea.

That I did so was a slice of luck, as, otherwise, the fuselage would probably have been ripped up, and the machine capsized.

When the floats smacked the water, we got quite a bump, and a decided jar in the nape of our necks.

Fortunately, however, the under-carriage struts retained their rigidity and did not buckle, and the seaplane rode the water right way up.

I will not worry the reader with a technical explanation of the trouble which had befallen our engine. Sufficient to state that it was of so serious a nature as to preclude us from any attempt at "patching her up."

"Do you know where we are?" inquired the pilot, after we had heartily chorused a round of expletives appropriate to such an eventuality. I shook my head.

It must be remembered we had been travelling through fog most of the journey, and therefore could not spot the regular aids to maritime aerial pilotage, such as lightvessels, sandbanks, buoys, and coast contours. In addition to this there are always air currents about, to counteract a dead compass-reckoning alone.

By taking the mean of our calculations, however, we were eventually able to place a finger on the approximate area where we believed ourselves to be on the chart.

The result was anything but encouraging. We were at least fifty miles from the shores of England, and in a neighbourhood devoid of all shipping, even in times of peace. What was worse, it was gradually borne in upon us that we were perilously near, if not actually in, a most extensive mine-field!

Personally, I was feeling anything but buoyant, and the reason is not far to seek. I had had the middle watch (12.4 a.m.) in the wireless cabin ashore the previous night. A report then came through that there was "something buzzing"—hostile submarines scudding round, or Zeppelins or other aircraft—and I had the wireless of half-a-dozen machines to overhaul, and superintend their going off. Then my own turn came, and, minus breakfast or a bite of anything, off I went, having had no food since the previous afternoon at five. Worse still, I had not so much as a bite of "grub" about me, or even a smoke.

The pilot went through his pockets, and discovered one solitary cigarette resting in state in his case. Being a sportsman, as well as a companion in misfortune, he offered it to me, and, on my emphatic refusal, halved it. So, we both lit up whilst we reviewed the situation.

I don't believe I ever treated a smoke with greater care than I did that half-cigarette. For aught I knew it might be my last.

When we had finished our cogitations the joint result of our thinking was by no means hopeful.

2— S. O. S." Message on Machine Gun

A strong sun was beginning to shine through the intense heat-haze, and the glare of the water was very trying.

At regular intervals, I fired off a Very's light, with the idea of attracting attention. As the coloured projectiles curved high into the air and plunged downwards, so did our hopes seem to rise and fall.

When my Very's cartridges were exhausted, I commenced a series of "S.O.S." messages in the Morse code on the machine-gun. The nickel bullets of two trays of Mark VII. ammunition had winged through the heavy air before we realised the practical futility of it all.

We therefore kept the remainder of our gun magazines intact, as also a brace of heavy service revolvers, 455 calibre, fully loaded.

We were not to know what might crop up at any moment. A Taube might find us and swoop down for bombing practice, or to make an easy prey. We could not in any event be taken prisoners by hostile aircraft, as there would be no space for us in a machine already full.

At any moment, too, a U-boat might pop up and either make a target of us for their quick-firer or take us in tow for the Belgian coast, which was uncomfortably near at hand.

However, come what might, we were in a mood to fight to a finish.

Unfortunately, my wireless transmitter was worked from the engine direct, otherwise I might have rigged up an extempore aerial from the spare reel carried, and sent a "S.O.S." from accumulators.

It is doubtful if such a scheme would have proved effective, but it would have been worth trying. But in the circumstances, I was helpless.

The heat was now simply awful, the sea dead calm. We had taken off our leather coats long since, and now rigged them up across the fuselage overhead, for shelter from the sun's rays.

Presently it became so hot and stuffy on the seats that both the pilot and myself took our boots and trousers off, climbed down on the floats, and stretched ourselves along them in the comparative shelter of the wings and fuselage body.

The stern part of the floats was, of course, submerged, so we lay with our lower limbs under water, and felt cooler. This we did for about three hours, each of which seemed an age.

What with the heat and the want of food, which caused a dull throbbing in my temples, by noon I was in such a state that I did not care what happened to us.

The pilot (poor chap) had only recently been married, and he rattled along continually about his young wife.

I have no wish to be in like straits again, but if such a misfortune should happen, I earnestly trust I shall not have the misfortune to be beside a young fellow newly wedded! In the long weary time we spent together, I had the whole of his history, from childhood to courtship, and I suppose he had mine!

What surprised us was the great number of logs floating about. Apparently, a timber boat had foundered somewhere close by.

Every log that hove in sight through the haze we thought was a ship. It was a terrible time.

At intervals, we either heard—or imagined we did—the engines of aircraft. Sometimes they seemed all around us; sometimes a long way off.

"Our only chance is a relief seaplane being sent after us," said the pilot. "Otherwise we are done for!"

There was precious little chance of us ever being spotted, we reckoned, owing to the extremely low visibility.

At least a dozen times, as the day wore on, we heard the unmistakable roar of aircraft, and it was torture to listen to them.

"It's coming nearer. They will see us!" the pilot would cry, hopefully.

Then the sound would recede into the distance, and we would become despondent again.

3—We were Floating Over Dynamite

It was extremely irritating, whilst anxiously following these sounds with straining ears, to hear the swish, swish of the water across the floats, the ripple as it rejoined the ocean again, and the creak, creak of the great wings as we rose and fell with a squelch on the gentle undulations of a swell.

These sounds eventually developed into a perfect nightmare. Every swish and creak seemed to pierce our brains.

Eventually we climbed up into the seats again for a while and stared our eyes out scanning the horizon with our powerful glasses. Every piece of flotsam seen we dubbed a boat, till it drifted near enough to make out detail.

The wind got up a little and died down again, but it shifted the haze somewhat.

In the afternoon, we saw a sight which gladdened our hearts.

High up to the nor'-west, and dropping towards us, was a bird-like machine. Nearer and nearer it came, till we could hear the engines clearly. Soon we identified her marks, which set our fears at rest. It was a British 'plane.

We sprang up, gesticulated wildly, and fired a few pistol-shots just to relieve our excitement.

She was a rescue seaplane from our own base, it appeared, and presently she dropped on the water beside us and "taxied" as close as she might.

Her pilot steered within twenty yards or so of us, and the observer heaved overboard in our direction a huge vacuum flask.

Then, without stopping their engine, and waving cheerily, they droned along the surface and tilted into the air again. We watched her until the machine became a mere speck and finally faded into the blue.

Then, and not till then, we remembered the flask. We were fated never to taste its contents, however, for it floated past out of reach, in the midst of a great school of giant jellyfish.

I have never been stung by one of these loathsome-looking creatures, and I had no desire to be on this occasion. Neither had the pilot, so the bottle floated out of sight without giving us anything but moral support.

After this interlude, our long impatient wait recommenced. The episode had instilled hope into us, but the hours seemed to drag more heavily than ever. There was nothing but sea on every hand—a great circular expanse of glaring, shimmering water.

Presently schools of porpoises began to put in an appearance, sporting about in their own unmistakable style. There must have been hundreds of them. One group frolicked close around us, and several times a glossy black tail caught one or other of the floats a resounding smack.

The fabric of these floats is exceedingly frail, and we were rather concerned about them. It seemed a pity to shoot the playful creatures, particularly as their antics created a diversion, but we trembled for the safety of the floats every time they were struck.

As the tide went down, several dark, spheroidal objects commenced bobbing up by twos to the surface—on our starboard beam, as we were floating at that time.

Through our glasses we could spot scores more of them in the distance. No need to tell one another what they were. We knew—deadly contact mines!

The nearest pair were only a matter of half a cable's length away, and presently our worst ordeal commenced.

We were drifting towards them with the ebbing tide, and were now on the fringe of the great mine-field, perhaps the most extensive ever laid. Once in among those floating engines of death we should have a lively time.

It was with no very pleasant thoughts that we considered this new danger. I might have turned the machine gun on the mines, but there was the risk of exploding instead of sinking them, and if one went off it was fairly safe to assume that its mate, a couple of fathoms away, would detonate in sympathy. I presume that this is the underlying idea of distributing mines in this fashion.

During the next four hours, these horrid death-traps gave us a terribly anxious time. We had some very narrow shaves, for at low-water hundreds were in sight, and as the seaplane drifted along we were powerless to avoid them.

The pilot got on one float and I got on the other, and once or twice we actually had to ward the mines off with our bare hands in order to keep them from knocking against the machine. Had one of them done so this story would never have been written. Fending off the mines was a ticklish operation, as you may suppose. Great care had to be observed in exerting our strength, and we had to place our hands on parts of the casing of the mine that were devoid of horns, or between two horns, if it was not floating high enough. While engaged in this delightful occupation I went overboard twice, but managed to scramble back safely without getting into trouble with the mines.

Once a mine went off. It was too far away, however, for us to see what caused the explosion. It is not improbable that a luckless porpoise might have bent a horn in one of its leaps.

At length, to our heartfelt relief, the tide turned, and the mines began to disappear under the water again.

By that time, we were drifting nearly the opposite way again, carried along by the flood-tide.

4—An Aeroplane Comes to Rescue

Six o'clock came, by our chronometer—seven p.m. summer time—and we were still intact, having for about ten hours been dependent on our frail seaplane floats for buoyancy. Had the sea risen at all, even to a decent cat's paw, we should have been below the surface long ere this.

It was shortly after six o'clock, when—burnt almost black by the sun, with parched throats and swollen tongues—we heard the sound of a propeller chugging away at no great distance. The haze had thickened again as the sun moved west, and at first, we could see nothing. In fact, we both thought we were dreaming.

But there was no mistake. The chugging and throbbing grew louder and louder, and I fired three single pistol-shots into the air at intervals. Thereupon the sound intensified, and out of the haze ploughed a trim little armed motor-launch—officially known as an "M.L."

She crept alongside very gingerly, lowered her dinghy, and took us off. Then she made fast a line to the seaplane, and took her in tow at a good seven or eight knots.

We were heartily welcomed by the bluff sailormen aboard.

Curiously enough, I did not feel thirst so badly as hunger. I am not of a thirsty nature at any time, and perhaps that accounted for it.

The first mouthful of food was torture; it seemed to rasp the skin off my throat. After that I ate ravenously. It was the first touch of real hunger I had known, and after the experience, I vowed that if it lay in my power I would never again see a poor beggar go hungry.

When our bodily wants had been attended to we settled down to a comfortable smoke in the ward-room. The skipper, a Lieutenant R.N.R., told us he had just made up his mind he was not going to venture another fathom farther when he heard our shots. Owing to the proximity of the mine-field he had been very anxious.

After our smoke, we turned in for a sleep which only terminated when the "M.L." reached the shores of Old England and her diesel oil-engines ceased throbbing! This was long after midnight.

They say our little experience has left its mark on us, but personally I feel as fit as ever.

The Ghastly Havoc Wrought by the Air-Demons
By Logan Marshall

The Horror of Bomb-Dropping

Ten years ago, (as at 1920), the dropping of bombs from balloons was still considered an illegitimate form of warfare, involving danger to non-combatants, and was under the ban of the Geneva Convention. At The Hague Peace Conference the Germans refused to abstain from bomb-dropping, and other nations followed suit. According to the German conception of war, civilians in the theatre of operations must take their chance of being killed, but must not shoot back under pain of summary execution. The horrors which this theory has added to war have proved only too real, but, so far as bomb-dropping is concerned, the reality has so far fallen short of anticipations. The great Zeppelins, capable of carrying a ton of explosives, have practically been frightened out of the air by the new anti-aircraft guns; and, except for one instance at Antwerp, bomb-dropping has been confined to aeroplanes.

Now, in the first place, an aeroplane can carry only a limited weight of bomb—say, two hundred pounds; and in the second place, it is extraordinarily difficult to hit anything with them. If the airman could hover over his target and take deliberate aim, he might be more dangerous; as it is, the German airman finds a cathedral hardly a big enough mark.

The British airmen, at Düsseldorf and Lake Constance, adopted a different plan from the Germans; instead of dropping bombs from a great height, they made a steep "*vol piqué*" down on to the target, turned sharply up again, and dropped the bomb at the moment when the plane was checked by the elevator. This plan is more dangerous,

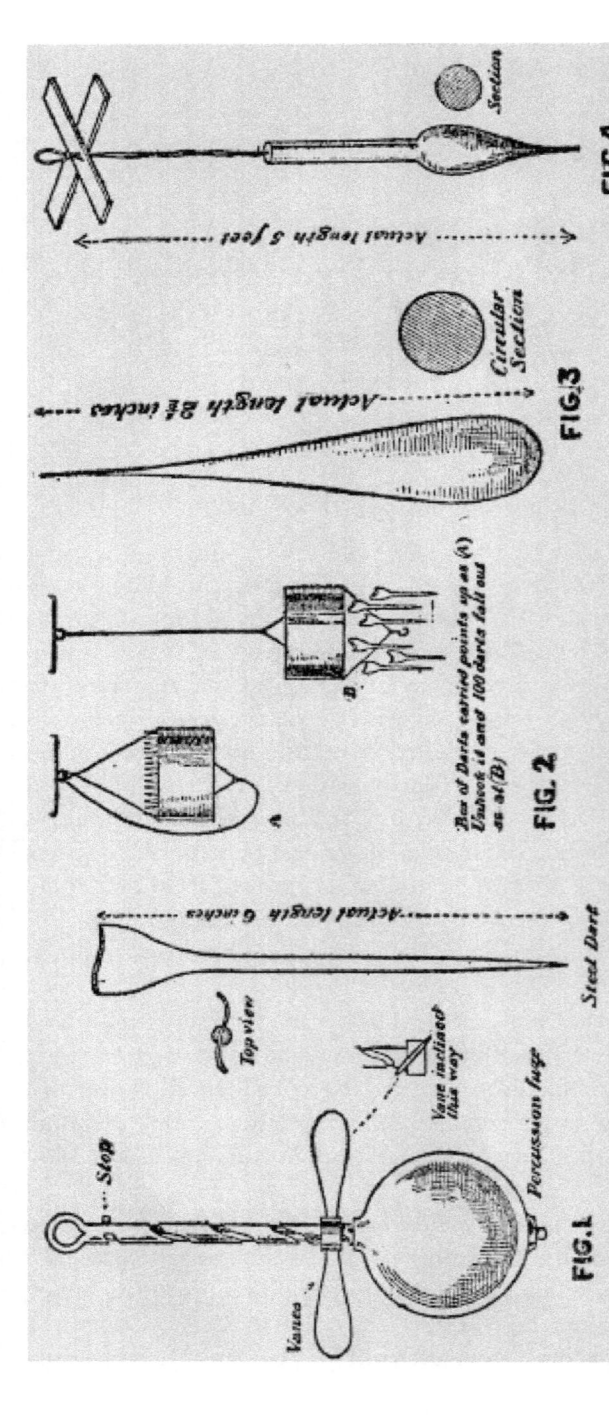

TYPES OF AIR-CRAFT WEAPONS.

Fig. 1.—An aeroplane bomb containing 12 lbs. of tetranitranilin, with a screw stem up which the vanes travel in flight and thus "arm" the fuse. Fig. 2.—Steel dart and boxes of darts used by Taube aeroplanes over Paris, showing how they are inverted and released. Fig. 3.—A French "arrow bullet"; very light, but able to kill a man from a height of 1,800 feet. Fig. 4.—A French aerial torpedo used by aeroplanes against Zeppelins, exploding when it has pierced an air-ship's envelope and is suddenly arrested by the wooden cross.

but affords a better chance of hitting.

Kinds of Bombs

Various kinds of bombs are used for dropping from aeroplanes. A simple pattern shown in Fig. 1 consists of a thin spherical shell of steel, containing twelve pounds of tetranitranilin, which is an explosive more powerful than melinite. The stem of the bomb, by which it is handled, has an external screw-thread, and carries a pair of vanes. While in the position shown, the bomb is harmless, but as it drops, the vanes screw themselves up to the top of the stem till they press against the stop. This, by mean of a rod passing down the centre of the stem, "arms" or prepares the fuse seen at the bottom of the bomb, so that it acts at the slightest touch, even on the wing of another aeroplane. The fuse effects the explosion of the burster by means of a primer of azide of lead, which causes the tetranitranilin to detonate with great violence. The whole bomb weighs twenty-two pounds, and an aeroplane usually carries six of them.

The Italians, in their campaign in Tripoli, used similar bombs, but without the special device for rendering the fuse sensitive. These were not a success, as many of them failed to explode in the desert sand, and the Arabs used to collect them and throw them into the Italian trenches at night.

Steel Darts

The Taube aeroplanes, when they flew over Paris, used sometimes to drop steel darts pointed at one end and flattened and feathered at the other, as shown in Fig. 2. These were put up in boxes of a hundred, so that when the box was released from its hook, it turned over and released the darts.

"Arrow Bullets" and Aerial Torpedoes

The "arrow bullet" shown in Fig. 3 is a French device; though weighing only three-quarters of an ounce, its peculiar shape enables it to acquire a high velocity, so that it will kill a man when dropped from a height of six hundred yards. An aerial torpedo carried by French aeroplanes for the destruction of Zeppelins is shown in Fig. 4; it contains a powerful charge of explosive and a fuse, to which the suspending-wire is connected. When dropped on a Zeppelin, the needle-pointed torpedo pierces the envelope and gas-chamber, but the wooden cross is arrested and the sudden jerk on the suspending-wire sets the fuse in action, causing the certain destruction of the airship. The torpedo would be too dangerous to handle, but the French have an ingenious device which renders it perfectly safe until it is dropped.

Machine Guns in Aircraft

Various attempts have been made to mount machine guns on aeroplanes, but the operator, in his narrow seat, has hardly space to point a machine gun in any direction except straight to his front. The American Curtis machine gun exhibited at Olympia is the most efficient form yet produced, but at present the airman seems to prefer an automatic rifle. Even in the early days of the war, Sir John French was able to report that British airmen had disposed of no less than five of the enemy's aircraft with this weapon.

The Zeppelins are well armed with machine guns, carrying one in each of the two cars, and one on top of the structure. Access is had to the latter by means of a shaft and ladder which passes up through the gas-chambers.

Accuracy in Dropping Bombs

The Zeppelins have elaborate bomb-dropping apparatus with which it should be theoretically possible to drop a bomb with great accuracy, but on the occasion when it was tried at Antwerp, the Germans met with no great success. The principle of the bomb-dropping device is as follows: A sort of camera, pointed vertically downwards, is used, and an observer notes the speed with which an object on the ground passes across the field, and the direction in which it appears to move. He then reads the height of the airship from the barometer, which gives the time taken by the bomb to fall, say fifteen seconds for 3,500 feet. He has now to calculate, from the data given by the camera-observation, the allowance to be made for speed and leeway for fifteen seconds of fall, and to point his sighting-tube accordingly. The air-ship is steered to windward of the target, and at the moment when the target (say, the second funnel of a dreadnaught) appears on the cross wires, the nine hundred-pound bomb is dropped, and the ship goes to the bottom.

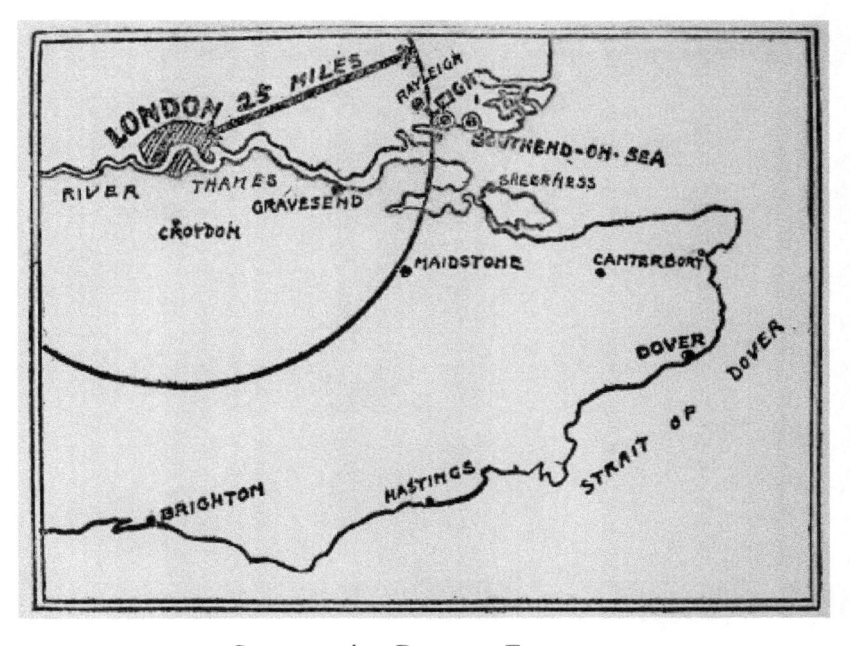

SCENE OF AIR RAID ON ENGLAND.
Leigh, shown on the map, is only twenty-five miles from the British capital, and South End just five miles further on. The fleet of Zeppelins, or aeroplanes, or both, it will be seen, got uncomfortably close to the British metropolis.

"Flying for France"—Hero Tales of Battles in the Air

With the American Escadrille at Verdun
Told by James R. McConnell, Sergeant-Pilot in the French Flying Corps

The story of how Jim McConnell, the young North Carolinian, went to France and gave his life to the cause of human liberty, is a noble tribute to young Americanism. His heroic deeds at the battle of Verdun when he fought with the American aviators in a sea of clouds is a classic that would do credit to the ancient Greeks. A comrade tells this story:

> One day in January, 1915, I saw Jim McConnell in front of the Court House at Carthage, North Carolina. 'Well,' he said, 'I am all fixed up and I am leaving on Wednesday.' 'Where for?' I asked. 'I have got a job to drive an ambulance in France' was his answer. And then he went on to tell me, first, that as he saw it the greatest event of history was going on right at hand. 'These sand hills,' he said, 'will be here forever but the war won't—and so I am going.' So, he went. He joined the American Ambulance Service in the Vosges, was mentioned many times in the Orders of the Day for conspicuous bravery in saving wounded under fire, and received the much-coveted *Croix de Guerre*.

As a Sergeant-Pilot in the Lafayette Escadrille of American Aviators, McConnell was killed in March, 1917, in an encounter with two Boche-driven aeroplanes. It was his hope that he might lead a United States Army Aero Corps on the French front. He, indeed, had a part in great deeds and left the best description yet published of the most terrific battle in the war up to the time of his death. His book, titled *Flying for France*, was published in 1917. Some of his experiences are among the following collection of stories.

1—Story of the American Airmen

Beneath the canvas of a huge hangar mechanicians are at work on the motor of an airplane. Outside, on the borders of an aviation field, others loiter awaiting their aerial charge's return from the sky. Near the hangar stands a hut-shaped tent. In front of it several short-winged biplanes are lined up; inside it three or four young men are lolling in wicker chairs.

They wear the uniform of French army aviators. These uniforms, and the grim-looking machine guns mounted on the upper planes of the little aircraft, are the only warlike note in a pleasantly peaceful scene. The war seems very remote. It is hard to believe that the greatest of all battles—Verdun—rages only twenty-five miles to the north, and that the field and hangars and mechanicians and aviators and airplanes are all playing a part therein.

Suddenly there is the distant hum of a motor. One of the pilots emerges from the tent and gazes fixedly up into the blue sky. He points, and one glimpses a black speck against the blue, high overhead. The sound of the motor ceases, and the speck grows larger. It moves earthward in steep dives and circles, and as it swoops closer, takes on the shape of an airplane. Now one can make out the red, white, and blue circles under the wings which mark a French war-plane, and the distinctive insignia of the pilot on its sides.

"*Ton patron arrive!*" one mechanician cries to another. "Your boss is coming!"

The machine dips sharply over the top of a hangar, straightens out again near the earth at a dizzy speed a few feet above it and, losing momentum in a surprisingly short time, hits the ground with tail and wheels. It bumps along a score of yards and then, its motor whirring again, turns, rolls toward the hangar, and stops. A human form, enveloped in a species of garment for all the world like a diver's suit, and further adorned with goggles and a leather hood, rises unsteadily in the cockpit, clambers awkwardly overboard and slides down to *terra firma*.

A group of soldiers, enjoying a brief holiday from the trenches in a cantonment near the field, straggle forward and gather timidly about the airplane, listening open-mouthed for what its rider is about to say.

"Hell!" mumbles that gentleman, as he starts divesting himself of his flying garb.

"What's wrong now?" inquires one of the tenants of the tent.

"Everything, or else I've gone nutty," is the indignant reply, delivered while disengaging a leg from its Teddy Bear trousering. "Why, I emptied my whole roller on a Boche this morning, point blank at not fifteen metres off. His machine gun quit firing and his propeller wasn't turning and yet the darn fool just hung up there as if he were tied to a cloud. Say, I was so sure I had him it made me sore—felt like running into him and yelling, 'Now, you fall, you bum!'"

The eyes of the *poilus* register surprise. Not a word of this dialogue, delivered in purest American, is intelligible to them. Why is an aviator in a French uniform speaking a foreign tongue, they mutually ask themselves? Finally, one of them, a little chap in a uniform long since bleached of its horizon-blue colour by the mud of the firing line, whisperingly interrogates a mechanician as to the identity of these strange air folk.

"But they are the Americans, my old one," the latter explains with noticeable condescension.

Marvelling afresh, the infantrymen demand further details. They learn that they are witnessing the return of the American Escadrille—composed of Americans who have volunteered to fly for France for the duration of the war—to their station near Bar-le-Duc, twenty-five miles south of Verdun, from a flight over the battle front of the Meuse. They have barely had time to digest this knowledge when other dots appear in the sky, and one by one turn into airplanes as they wheel downward. Finally, all six of the machines that have been aloft are back on the ground and the American Escadrille has one more sortie over the German lines to its credit.

2—Story of the Personnel of the Escadrille

Like all worthwhile institutions, the American Escadrille, of which I have the honour of being a member, was of gradual growth. When the war began, it is doubtful whether anybody anywhere envisaged the possibility of an American entering the French aviation service. Yet, by the fall of 1915, scarcely more than a year later, there were six Americans serving as full-fledged pilots, and now, in the summer of 1916, the list numbers fifteen or more, with twice that number training for their pilot's license in the military aviation schools.

The pioneer of them all was William Thaw, of Pittsburg, who is today, (1920), the only American holding a commission in the French flying corps. Lieutenant Thaw, a flyer of considerable reputation in

America before the war, had enlisted in the Foreign Legion in August, 1914. With considerable difficulty he had himself transferred, in the early part of 1915, into aviation, and the autumn of that year found him piloting a Caudron biplane, and doing excellent observation work. At the same time, Sergeants Norman Prince, of Boston, and Elliot Cowdin, of New York—who were the first to enter the aviation service coming directly from the United States—were at the front on Voisin planes with a cannon mounted in the bow.

Sergeant Bert Hall, who signs from the Lone Star State and had got himself shifted from the Foreign Legion to aviation soon after Thaw, was flying a Nieuport fighting machine, and, a little later, instructing less-advanced students of the air in the Avord Training School. Hall's book *En l'air! (In the Air)* is republished by Leonaur. His particular chum in the Foreign Legion, James Bach, who also had become an aviator, had the distressing distinction soon after he reached the front of becoming the first American to fall into the hands of the enemy. Going to the assistance of a companion who had broken down in landing a spy in the German lines. Bach smashed his machine against a tree. Both he and his French comrade were captured, and Bach was twice court-martialled by the Germans on suspicion of being an American *franc-tieur*—the penalty for which is death! He was acquitted but of course still, (1920), languishes in a prison camp "somewhere in Germany."

The sixth of the original sextet was Adjutant Didier Masson, who did exhibition flying in the States until—Carranza having grown ambitious in Mexico—he turned his talents to spotting *los Federales* for General Obregon. When the real war broke out, Masson answered the call of his French blood and was soon flying and fighting for the land of his ancestors.

Of the other members of the *escadrille* Sergeant Givas Lufbery, American citizen and soldier, but dweller in the world at large, was among the earliest to wear the French airman's wings. Exhibition work with a French pilot in the Far East prepared him efficiently for the task of patiently unloading explosives on to German military centres from a slow-moving Voisin which was his first mount. Upon the heels of Lufbery came two more graduates of the Foreign Legion—Kiffin Rockwell, of Asheville, N. C, who had been wounded at Carency; Victor Chapman, of New York, who after recovering from his wounds became an airplane bomb-dropper and so caught the craving to become a pilot. At about this time one Paul Pavelka, whose birthplace was Madison, Conn., and who from the age of fifteen had sailed the seven seas, managed to slip out of the Foreign Legion into aviation and joined the other Americans at Pau.

There seems to be a fascination to aviation, particularly when it is coupled with fighting. Perhaps it's because the game is new, but more probably because as a rule nobody knows anything about it. Whatever be the reason, adventurous young Americans were attracted by it in rapidly increasing numbers. Many of them, of course, never got fascinated beyond the stage of talking about joining. Among the chaps serving with the American ambulance field sections a good many imaginations were stirred, and a few actually did enlist, when, toward the end of the summer of 1915, the Ministry of War, finding that the original American pilots had made good, grew more liberal in considering applications.

Chouteau Johnson, of New York; Lawrence Rumsey, of Buffalo; Dudley Hill, of Peekskill, N.Y.; and Clyde Balsley, of El Paso; one after another doffed the ambulance driver's khaki for the horizon-blue of the French flying corps. All of them had seen plenty of action, collecting the wounded under fire, but they were all tired of being non-combatant spectators. More or less the same feeling actuated me, I suppose. I had come over from Carthage, N. C, in January, 1915, and worked with an American ambulance section in the Bois-le-Prêtre. All along I had been convinced that the United States ought to aid in the struggle against Germany. With that conviction, it was plainly up to me to do more than drive an ambulance. The more I saw the splendour of the fight the French were fighting, the more I felt like an *embusqué*—what the British call a "shirker." So, I made up my mind to go into aviation.

A special channel had been created for the reception of applications from Americans, and my own was favourably replied to within a few days. It took four days more to pass through all the various departments, sign one's name to a few hundred papers, and undergo the physical examinations. Then I was sent to the aviation depot at Dijon and fitted out with a uniform and personal equipment. The next stop was the school at Pau, where I was to be taught to fly. My elation at arriving there was second only to my satisfaction at being a French soldier. It was a vast improvement, I thought, to the American Ambulance.

Talk about forming an all-American flying unit, or *escadrille*, was rife while I was at Pau. What with the pilots already breveted, and the *élèves*, or pupils in the training-schools, there were quite enough of our compatriots to man the dozen airplanes in one *escadrille*. Every day somebody "had it absolutely straight" that we were to become a unit at the front, and every other day the report turned out to be untrue. But at last, in the month of February, our dream came true. We learned that a captain had actually been assigned to command an American Escadrille and that the Americans at the front had been recalled and placed under his orders. Soon afterward we *élèves* got another delightful thrill.

3—Story of the Fliers in Training

Thaw, Prince, Cowdin, and the other veterans were training on the Nieuport! That meant the American Escadrille was to fly the Nieuport—the best type of *avion de chasse*—and hence would be a fighting unit. It is necessary to explain parenthetically here that French military aviation, generally speaking, is divided into three groups—the *avions de chasse* or airplanes of pursuit, which are used to hunt down enemy aircraft or to fight them off; *avions de bombardement*, big, unwieldy monsters for use in bombarding raids; and *avions de rélage*, cumbersome creatures designed to regulate artillery fire, take photographs, and do scout duty. The Nieuport is the smallest, fastest-rising, fastest-moving biplane in the French service. It can travel no miles an hour, and is a one-man apparatus with a machine gun mounted on its roof and fired by the pilot with one hand while with the other and his feet he operates his controls. The French call their Nieuport pilots the "aces" of the air. No wonder we were tickled to be included in that august brotherhood!

Before the American Escadrille became an established fact, Thaw and Cowdin, who had mastered the Nieuport, managed to be sent to the Verdun front. While there Cowdin was credited with having brought down a German machine and was proposed for the *Médaille Militaire*, the highest decoration that can be awarded a non-commissioned officer or private.

After completing his training, receiving his military pilot's brevet, and being perfected on the type of plane he is to use at the front, an aviator is ordered to the reserve headquarters near Paris to await his call. Kiffin Rockwell and Victor Chapman had been there for months, and I had just arrived, when on the 16th of April orders came for the Americans to join their *escadrille* at Luxeuil, in the Vosges.

The rush was breathless! Never were flying clothes and fur coats drawn from the quartermaster, belongings packed, and red tape in the various administrative bureaux unfurled, with such headlong haste. In a few hours we were aboard the train, panting, but happy. Our party consisted of Sergeant Prince, and Rockwell, Chapman, and myself, who were only corporals at that time. We were joined at Luxeuil by Lieutenant Thaw and Sergeants Hall and Cowdin.

For the veterans, our arrival at the front was devoid of excitement; for the three neophytes—Rockwell, Chapman, and myself—it was the beginning of a new existence, the entry into an unknown world. Of course, Rockwell and Chapman had seen plenty of warfare on the ground, but warfare in the air was as novel to them as to me. For us all it contained unlimited possibilities for initiative and service to France, and for them it must have meant, too, the restoration of personality lost during those months in the trenches with the Foreign Legion. Rockwell summed it up characteristically.

"Well, we're off for the races," he remarked. . . .

On our arrival at Luxeuil we were met by Captain Thénault, the French commander of the American Escadrille—officially known as No. 124, by the way—and motored to the aviation field in one of the staff cars assigned to us. (Georges Thénault's book *The Story of the Lafayette Escadrille* is republished by Leonaur). I enjoyed that ride. Lolling back against the soft leather cushions, I recalled how in my apprenticeship days at Pau I had had to walk six miles for my laundry. . . .

Rooms were assigned to us in a villa adjoining the famous hot baths of Luxeuil, where Caesar's *cohorts* were wont to besport themselves. We messed with our officers, Captain Thénault and Lieutenant de Laage de Mux, at the best hotel in town. An automobile was always on hand to carry us to the field. I began to wonder whether I was a summer resorter instead of a soldier.

Among the pilots who had welcomed us with open arms, we discovered the famous Captain Happe, commander of the Luxeuil bombardment group. The doughty bomb-dispenser, upon whose head the Germans have set a price, was in his quarters. After we had been introduced, he pointed to eight little boxes arranged on a table.

"They contain *Croix de Guerre* for the families of the men I lost on my last trip," he explained, and he added: "It's a good thing you're here to go along with us for protection. There are lots of Boches in this sector."

I thought of the luxury we were enjoying: our comfortable beds, baths, and motorcars, and then I recalled the ancient custom of giving a man selected for the sacrifice a royal time of it before the appointed day. . . .

4—Story of the First Sortie in the Clouds

The memory of the first sortie we made as an *escadrille* will always remain fresh in my mind because it was also my first trip over the lines. We were to leave at six in the morning. Captain Thénault pointed out on his aerial map the route we were to follow. Never having flown over this region before, I was afraid of losing myself. Therefore, as it is easier to keep other airplanes in sight when one is above them, I began climbing as rapidly as possible, meaning to trail along in the wake of my companions. Unless one has had practice in flying in formation, however, it is hard to keep in contact. The diminutive *avians de chasse* are the merest pin points against the great sweep of landscape below and the limitless heavens above.

The air was misty and clouds were gathering. Ahead there seemed a barrier of them. Although as I looked down the ground showed plainly, in the distance everything was hazy. Forging up above the mist, at 7,000 feet, I lost the others altogether. Even when they are not closely joined, the clouds, seen from immediately above, appear as a solid bank of white. The spaces between are indistinguishable. It is like being in an Arctic ice field.

To the south I made out the Alps. Their glittering peaks projected up through the white sea about me like majestic icebergs. Not a single plane was visible anywhere, and I was growing very uncertain about my position. My splendid isolation had become oppressive, when, one by one, the others began bobbing up above the cloud level, and I had company again.

We were over Belfort and headed for the trench lines. The cloud banks dropped behind, and below us we saw the smiling plain of Alsace stretching eastward to the Rhine. It was distinctly pleasurable, flying over this conquered land. Following the course of the canal that runs to the Rhine, I sighted, from a height of 13,000 feet over Dannemarie, a series of brown, woodworm-like tracings on the ground—the trenches!

My attention was drawn elsewhere almost immediately, however. Two balls of black smoke had suddenly appeared close to one of the machines ahead of me, and with the same disconcerting abruptness similar balls began to dot the sky above, below, and on all sides of us. We were being shot at with shrapnel. It was interesting to watch the flash of the bursting shells, and the attendant smoke puffs—black, white, or yellow, depending on the kind of shrapnel used. The roar of the motor drowned the noise of the explosions. Strangely enough, my feelings about it were wholly impersonal.

We turned north after crossing the lines. Mulhouse seemed just below us, and I noted with a keen sense of satisfaction our invasion of real German territory. The Rhine, too, looked delightfully accessible. As we continued northward I distinguished the twin lakes of Gérardmer sparkling in their emerald setting. Where the lines crossed the Hartmannsweilerkopf there were little spurts of brown smoke as shells burst in the trenches. One could scarcely pick out the old city of Thann from among the numerous neighbouring villages, so tiny it seemed in the valley's mouth. I had never been higher than 7,000 feet and was unaccustomed to reading country from a great altitude.

It was also bitterly cold, and even in my fur-lined combination I was shivering. I noticed, too, that I had to take long, deep breaths in the rarefied atmosphere. Looking downward at a certain angle, I saw what at first I took to be a round, shimmering pool of water. It was simply the effect of the sunlight on the congealing mist. We had been keeping an eye out for German machines since leaving our lines, but none had shown up. It wasn't surprising, for we were too many.

Only four days later, however, Rockwell brought down the *escadrille's* first plane in his initial aerial combat. He was flying alone when, over Thann, he came upon a German on reconnaissance. He dived and the German turned toward his own lines, opening fire from a long distance. Rockwell kept straight after him.

Then, closing to within thirty yards, he pressed on the release of his machine gun, and saw the enemy gunner fall backward and the pilot crumple up sideways in his seat. The plane flopped downward and crashed to earth just behind the German trenches. Swooping close to the ground Rockwell saw its debris burning away brightly. He had turned the trick with but four shots and only one German bullet had struck his Nieuport. An observation post telephoned the news before Rockwell's return, and he got a great welcome. All Luxeuil smiled upon him—particularly the girls. But he couldn't stay to enjoy his popularity. The *escadrille* was ordered to the sector of Verdun.

While in a way we were sorry to leave Luxeuil, we naturally didn't regret the chance to take part in the aerial activity of the world's greatest battle. The night before our departure some German aircraft destroyed four of our tractors and killed six men with bombs, but even that caused little excitement compared with going to Verdun. We would get square with the Boches over Verdun, we thought—it is impossible to chase airplanes at night, so the raiders made a safe getaway. . . .

The fast-flowing stream of troops, and the distressing number of ambulances brought realisation of the near presence of a gigantic battle.

Within a twenty-mile radius of the Verdun front aviation camps abound. Our *escadrille* was listed on the schedule with the other fighting units, each of which has its specified flying hours, rotating so there is always an *escadrille de chasse* over the lines. A field wireless to enable us to keep track of the movements of enemy planes became part of our equipment.

Lufberry joined us a few days after our arrival. He was followed by Johnson and Balsley, who had been on the air guard over Paris. Hill and Rumsey came next, and after them Masson and Pavelka. Nieuports were supplied them from the nearest depot, and as soon as they had mounted their instruments and machine guns, they were on the job with the rest of us. Fifteen Americans are or have been members of the American Escadrille, but there have never been so many as that on duty at any one time.

5—Story of the Battles in the Skies

Before we were fairly settled at Bar-le-Duc, Hall brought down a German observation craft and Thaw a *Fokker*. Fights occurred on almost every sortie. The Germans seldom cross into our territory, unless on a bombarding jaunt, and thus practically all the fighting takes place on their side of the line. Thaw dropped his *Fokker* in the morning, and on the afternoon of the same day there was a big combat far behind the German trenches. Thaw was wounded in the arm, and an explosive bullet detonating on Rockwell's wind-shield tore several gashes in his face. Despite the blood which was blinding him Rockwell managed to reach an aviation field and land. Thaw, whose wound bled profusely, landed in a dazed condition just within our lines. He was too weak to walk, and French soldiers carried him to a field dressing-station, whence he was sent to Paris for further treatment. Rockwell's wounds were less serious and he insisted on flying again almost immediately.

A week or so later Chapman was wounded. Considering the number of fights, he had been in, and the courage with which he attacked, it was a miracle he had not been hit before. He always fought against odds and far within the enemy's country. He flew more than any of us, never missing an opportunity to go up, and never coming down until his gasoline was giving out. His machine was a sieve of patched-up bullet holes. His nerve was almost superhuman and his devotion to the cause for which he fought sublime. The day he was wounded he attacked four machines. Swooping down from behind, one of them, a *Fokker*, riddled Chapman's plane. One bullet cut deep into his scalp, but Chapman, a master pilot, escaped from the trap, and fired several shots to show he was still safe. A stability control had been severed by a bullet. Chapman held the broken rod in one hand, managed his machine with the other, and succeeded in landing on a near-by aviation field. His wound was dressed, his machine repaired, and he immediately took the air in pursuit of some more enemies. He would take no rest, and with bandaged head continued to fly and fight.

The *escadrille's* next serious encounter with the foe took place a few days later. Rockwell, Balsley, Prince, and Captain Thénault were surrounded by a large number of Germans, who, circling about them, commenced firing at long range. Realizing their numerical inferiority, the Americans and their commander sought the safest way out by attacking the enemy machines nearest the French lines. Rockwell, Prince, and the captain broke through successfully, but Balsley found himself hemmed in. He attacked the German nearest him, only to receive an explosive bullet in his thigh. In trying to get away by a vertical dive his machine went into a corkscrew and swung over on its back. Extra cartridge rollers dislodged from their case hit his arms. He was tumbling straight toward the trenches, but by a supreme effort he regained control, righted the plane, and landed without disaster in a meadow just behind the firing line.

Soldiers carried him to the shelter of a near-by fort, and later he was taken to a field hospital, where he lingered for days between life and death. Ten fragments of the explosive bullet were removed from his stomach. He bore up bravely, and became the favourite of the wounded officers in whose ward he lay. When we flew over to see him they would say: *Il est un brave petit gars, l'aviateur américain.* (He's a brave little fellow, the American aviator.) On a shelf by his bed, done up in a handkerchief, he kept the pieces of bullet taken out of him, and under them some sheets of paper on which he was trying to write to his mother, back in El Paso.

Balsley was awarded the *Médaille Militaire* and the *Croix de Guerre*, but the honours scared him. He had seen them decorate officers in the ward before they died.

6—Story of Chapman's Last Fight

Then came Chapman's last fight. Before leaving, he had put two bags of oranges in his machine to take to Balsley, who liked to suck them to relieve his terrible thirst, after the day's flying was over. There was an aerial struggle against odds, far within the German lines, and Chapman, to divert their fire from his comrades, engaged several enemy airmen at once. He sent one tumbling to earth, and had forced the others off when two more swooped down upon him. Such a fight is a matter of seconds, and one cannot clearly see what passes. Lufberry and Prince, whom Chapman had defended so gallantly, regained the French lines.

They told us of the combat, and we waited on the field for Chapman's return. He was always the last in, so we were not much worried. Then a pilot from another fighting *escadrille* telephoned us, that he had seen a Nieuport falling. A little later the observer of a reconnaissance airplane called up and told us how he had witnessed Chapman's fall. The wings of the plane had buckled, and it had dropped like a stone he said.

We talked in lowered voices after that; we would read the pain in one another's eyes. If only it could have been someone else, was what we all thought, I suppose. To lose Victor was not an irreparable loss to us merely, but to France, and to the world as well. I kept thinking of him lying over there, and of the oranges he was taking to Balsley. As I left the field I caught sight of Victor's mechanician leaning against the end of our hangar. He was looking northward into the sky where his *patron* had vanished, and his face was very sad.

By this time Prince and Hall had been made adjutants, and we corporals transformed into sergeants. I frankly confess to a feeling of marked satisfaction at receiving that grade in the world's finest army. I was a far more important person, in my own estimation, than I had been as a second lieutenant in the militia at home. The next impressive event was the awarding of decorations. We had assisted at that ceremony for Cowdin at Luxeuil, but this time three of our messmates were to be honoured for the Germans they had brought down. Rockwell and Hall received the *Médaille Militaire* and the *Croix de Guerre*, and Thaw, being a lieutenant, the *Légion d'honneur* and another "palm" for the ribbon of the *Croix de Guerre* he had won previously. Thaw, who came up from Paris specially for the presentation, still carried his arm in a sling.

There were also decorations for Chapman, but poor Victor, who so often had been cited in the Orders of the Day, was not on hand to receive them.

7—Story of the Morning Sortie Over Verdun

Our daily routine goes on with little change. Whenever the weather permits—that is, when it isn't raining, and the clouds aren't too low—we fly over the Verdun battlefield at the hours dictated by General Headquarters. As a rule, the most successful sorties are those in the early morning.

We are called while it's still dark Sleepily I try to reconcile the French orderly's muttered, *C'est l'heure, monsieur,* that rouses me from slumber, with the strictly American words and music of "When That Midnight Choo Choo Leaves for Alabam'" warbled by a particularly wide-awake pilot in the next room. A few minutes later, having swallowed some coffee, we motor to the field. The east is turning grey as the hangar curtains are drawn apart and our machines trundled out by the mechanicians. All the pilots whose planes are in commission—save those remaining behind on guard—prepare to leave. We average from four to six on a sortie, unless too many flights have been ordered for that day, in which case only two or three go out at a time.

Now the east is pink, and overhead the sky has changed from grey to pale blue. It is light enough to fly. We don our fur-lined shoes and combinations, and adjust the leather flying hoods and goggles. A good deal of conversation occurs—perhaps because, once aloft, there's nobody to talk to.

"Eh, you," one pilot cries jokingly to another, "I hope some Boche just ruins you this morning, so I won't have to pay you the fifty *francs* you won from me last night!"

This financial reference concerns a poker game.

"You do, do you?" replies the other as he swings into his machine. "Well, I'd be glad to pass up the fifty to see you landed by the Boches. You'd make a fine sight walking down the street of some German town in those wooden shoes and pyjama pants. Why don't you dress yourself? Don't you know an aviator's supposed to look chief?"

A sartorial eccentricity on the part of one of our colleagues is here referred to.

The raillery is silenced by a deafening roar as the motors are tested. Quiet is briefly restored, only to be broken by a series of rapid explosions incidental to the trying out of machine guns. You loudly inquire at what altitude we are to meet above the field.

"Fifteen hundred metres—go ahead!" comes an answering yell.

"*Essence et gas!* (Oil and gas!)" you call to your mechanician, adjusting your gasoline and air throttles while he grips the propeller.

"*Contact!*" he shrieks, and "*Contact!*" you reply. You snap on the switch, he spins the propeller, and the motor takes. Drawing forward out of line, you put on full, power, race across the grass and take the air. The ground drops as the hood slants up before you and you seem to be going more and more slowly as you rise. At a great height, you hardly realise you are moving. You glance at the clock to note the time of your departure, and at the oil gauge to see its throb. The altimeter registers 650 feet. You turn and look back at the field below and see others leaving.

In three minutes, you are at about 4,000 feet. You have been making wide circles over the field and watching the other machines. At 4,500 feet, you throttle down and wait on that level for your companions to catch up. Soon the *escadrille* is bunched and off for the lines. You begin climbing again, gulping to clear your ears in the changing pressure. Surveying the other machines, you recognise the pilot of each by the marks on its side—or by the way he flies. The distinguishing marks of the Nieuports are various and sometimes amusing. Bert Hall, for instance, has Bert painted on the left side of his plane and the same word reversed (as if spelled backward with the left hand) on the right—so an aviator passing him on that side at great speed will be able to read the name without difficulty, he says!

The country below has changed into a flat surface of varicoloured figures. Woods are irregular blocks of dark green, like daubs of ink spilled on a table; fields are geometrical designs of different shades of green and brown, forming in composite an ultra-cubist painting; roads are thin white lines, each with its distinctive windings and crossings—from which you determine your location. The higher you are the easier it is to read.

In about ten minutes you see the Meuse sparkling in the morning light, and on either side the long line of sausage-shaped observation balloons far below you. Red-roofed Verdun springs into view just beyond. There are spots in it where no red shows and you know what has happened there. In the green pasture land bordering the town, round flecks of brown indicate the shell holes. You cross the Meuse.

Immediately east and north of Verdun there lies a broad, brown band. From the Woevre plain it runs westward to the "S" bend in the Meuse, and on the left bank of that famous stream continues on into the Argonne Forest. Peaceful fields and farms and villages adorned that landscape a few months ago—when there was no Battle of Verdun. Now there is only that sinister brown belt, a strip of murdered Nature. It seems to belong to another world. Every sign of humanity has been swept away. The woods and roads have vanished like chalk wiped from a blackboard; of the villages, nothing remains but grey smears where stone walls have tumbled together.

The great forts of Douaumont and Vaux are outlined faintly, like the tracings of a finger in wet sand. One cannot distinguish any one shell crater, as one can on the pockmarked fields on either side. On the brown band the indentations are so closely interlocked that they blend into a confused mass of troubled earth. Of the trenches only broken, half-obliterated links are visible.

Columns of muddy smoke spurt up continually as high explosives tear deeper into this ulcered area. During heavy bombardment and attacks I have seen shells falling like rain. The countless towers of smoke remind one of Gustave Doré's picture of the fiery tombs of the arch-heretics in Dante's "Hell." A smoky pall covers the sector under fire, rising so high that at a height of 1,000 feet one is enveloped in its mist-like fumes. Now and then monster projectiles, hurtling through the air close by, leave one's plane rocking violently in their wake. Airplanes have been cut in two by them.

For us the battle passes in silence, the noise of one's motor deadening all other sounds. In the green patches behind the brown belt myriads of tiny flashes tell where the guns are hidden; and those flashes, and the smoke of bursting shells, are all we see of the fighting. It is a weird combination of stillness and havoc, the Verdun conflict viewed from the sky.

Far below us, the observation and range-finding planes circle over the trenches like gliding gulls. At a feeble altitude, they follow the attacking infantrymen and flash back wireless reports of the engagement. Only through them can communication be maintained when, under the barrier fire, wires from the front lines are cut. Sometimes it falls to our lot to guard these machines from Germans eager to swoop down on their backs. Sailing about high above a busy flock of them makes one feel like an old mother hen protecting her chicks....

Getting started is the hardest part of an attack. Once you have begun diving you're all right. The pilot just ahead turns tail up like a trout dropping back to water, and swoops down in irregular curves and circles. You follow at an angle so steep your feet seem to be holding you back in your seat. Now the black Maltese crosses on the German's wings stand out clearly. You think of him as some sort of big bug. Then you hear the rapid *tut-tut-tut* of his machine gun. The man that dived ahead of you becomes mixed up with the topmost German. He is so close it looks as if he had hit the enemy machine. You hear the *staccato* barking of his *mitrailleuse* and see him pass from under the German's tail.

The rattle of the gun that is aimed at you leaves you undisturbed. Only when the bullets pierce the wings a few feet off do you become uncomfortable. You see the gunner crouched down behind his weapon, but you aim at where the pilot ought to be—there are two men aboard the German craft—and press on the release hard. Your mitrailleuse hammers out a stream of bullets as you pass over and dive, nose down, to get out of range. Then, hopefully, you re-dress and look back at the foe. He ought to be dropping earthward at several miles a minute. As a matter of fact, however, he is sailing serenely on. They have an annoying habit of doing that, these Boches.

8—Story of a Fight Over Fort Douaumont

Rockwell, who attacked so often that he has lost all count, and who shoves his machine gun fairly in the faces of the Germans, used to swear their planes were armoured. Lieutenant de Laage, whose list of combats is equally extensive, has brought down only one. Hall, with three machines to his credit, has had more luck. Lufbery, who evidently has evolved a secret formula, has dropped four, according to official statistics, since his arrival on the Verdun front. Four "palms"—the record for the *escadrille*, glitter upon the ribbon of the *Croix de Guerre* accompanying his *Médaile Militaire*. (This book was written in the fall of 1915. Since that time many additional machines have been credited to the American flyers).

A pilot seldom has the satisfaction of beholding the result of his bull's-eye bullet. Rarely—so difficult it is to follow the turnings and twistings of the dropping plane—does he see his fallen foe strike the ground. Lufbery's last direct hit was an exception, for he followed all that took place from a balcony seat. I myself was in the "nigger-heaven," so I know. We had set out on a sortie together just before noon, one August day, and for the first time on such an occasion had lost each other over the lines. Seeing no Germans, I passed my time hovering over the French observation machines. Lufbery found one, however, and promptly brought it down. Just then I chanced to make a southward turn, and caught sight of an airplane falling out of the sky into the German lines.

As it turned over, it showed its white belly for an instant, then seemed to straighten out, and planed downward in big zigzags. The pilot must have gripped his controls even in death, for his craft did not tumble as most do. It passed between my line of vision and a wood, into which it disappeared. Just as I was going down to find out where it landed, I saw it again skimming across a field, and heading straight for the brown band beneath me. It was outlined against the shell-racked earth like a tiny insect, until just northwest of Fort Douaumont it crashed down upon the battlefield. A sheet of flame and smoke shot up from the tangled wreckage. For a moment or two I watched it burn; then I went back to the observation machines.

I thought Lufbery would show up and point to where the German had fallen. He failed to appear, and I began to be afraid it was he whom I had seen come down, instead of an enemy. I spent a worried hour before my return homeward. After getting back I learned that Lufbery was quite safe, having hurried in after the fight to report the destruction of his adversary before somebody else claimed him, which is only too frequently the case. Observation posts, however, confirmed Lufbery's story, and he was of course very much delighted. Nevertheless, at luncheon, I heard him murmuring, half to himself: "Those poor fellows."

The German machine gun operator, having probably escaped death in the air, must have had a hideous descent. Lufbery told us he had seen the whole thing, spiralling down after the German. He said he thought the German pilot must be a novice, judging from his manoeuvres. It occurred to me that he might have been making his first flight over the lines, doubtless full of enthusiasm about his career. Perhaps, dreaming of the Iron Cross and his Gretchen, he took a chance—and then swift death and a grave in the shell-strewn soil of Douaumont. . . .

9—Story of Prince's Aerial Fireworks

Now and then one of us will get ambitious to do something on his own account. Not long ago Norman Prince became obsessed with the idea of bringing down a German "sausage," as observation balloons are called. He had a special device mounted on his Nieuport for setting fire to the aerial frankfurters. Thus equipped he resembled an advance agent for Payne's fireworks more than an *aviator de chasse*.

Having carefully mapped the enemy "sausages," he would sally forth in hot pursuit whenever one was signalled at a respectable height. Poor Norman had a terrible time of it! Sometimes the reported "sausages" were not there when he arrived, and sometimes there was a super-abundancy of German airplanes on guard.

He stuck to it, however, and finally his appetite for "sausage" was satisfied. He found one just where it ought to be, swooped down upon it, and let off his fireworks with all the gusto of an American boy on the Fourth of July. When he looked again, the balloon had vanished. Prince's performance isn't so easy as it sounds, by the way. If, after the long dive necessary to turn the trick successfully, his motor had failed to retake, he would have fallen into the hands of the Germans.....

After dinner, the same scene invariably repeats itself, over the coffee in the "next room." At the big table, several sportive souls start a poker game, while at a smaller one two sedate spirits wrap themselves in the intricacies of chess. Captain Thénault labours away at the mess-room piano, or in lighter mood plays with Fram, his police dog. A phonograph grinds out the ancient query "Who Paid the Rent for Mrs. Rip Van Winkle?" or some other ragtime ditty. It is barely nine, however, when the movement in the direction of bed begins.

A few of us remain behind a little while, and the talk becomes more personal and more sincere. Only on such intimate occasions, I think, have I ever heard death discussed. Certainly, we are not indifferent to it. Not many nights ago one of the pilots remarked in a tired way:

"Know what I want? Just six months of freedom to go where and do what I like. In that time, I'd get everything I wanted out of life, and be perfectly willing to come back and be killed."

Then another, who was about to receive 2,000 *francs* from the American committee that aids us, as a reward for his many citations, chimed in.

"Well, I didn't care much before," he confessed, "but now with this money coming in I don't want to die until I've had the fun of spending it."

So, saying, he yawned and went up to bed.

10—Story of the Journey Toward the Somme

On the 12th of October, twenty small airplanes flying in a V formation, at such a height they resembled a flock of geese, crossed the river Rhine, where it skirts the plains of Alsace, and, turning north, headed for the famous Mauser works at Oberndorf. Following in their wake was an equal number of larger machines, and above these darted and circled swift fighting planes. The first group of aircraft was flown by British pilots, the second by French and three of the fighting planes by Americans in the French Aviation Division. It was a cosmopolitan collection that effected that successful raid.

We American pilots, who are grouped into one *escadrille*, had been fighting above the battlefield of Verdun from the 20th of May until orders came the middle of September for us to leave our airplanes, for a unit that would replace us, and to report at Le Bourget, the great Paris aviation centre.

The mechanics and the rest of the personnel left, as usual, in the *escadrille's* trucks with the material. For once the pilots did not take the aerial route but they boarded the Paris express at Bar-le-Duc with all the enthusiasm of schoolboys off for a vacation. They were to have a week in the capital! Where they were to go after that they did not know, but presumed it would be the Somme. As a matter of fact, the *escadrille* was to be sent to Luxeuil in the Vosges to take part in the Mauser raid.

Besides Captain Thénault and Lieutenant de Laage de Mieux, our French officers, the following American pilots were in the *escadrille* at this time: Lieutenant Thaw, who had returned to the front, even though his wounded arm had not entirely healed; Adjutants Norman Prince, Hall, Lufbery, and Masson; and Sergeants Kiffin Rockwell, Hill, Pavelka, Johnson, and Rumsey. I had been sent to a hospital at the end of August, because of a lame back resulting from a smash up in landing, and couldn't follow the *escadrille* until later.

Every aviation unit boasts several mascots. Dogs of every description are to be seen around the camps, but the Americans managed, during their stay in Paris, to add to their menagerie by the acquisition of a lion cub named "Whiskey." The little chap had been born on a boat crossing from Africa and was advertised for sale in France. Some of the American pilots chipped in and bought him.

He was a cute, bright-eyed baby lion who tried to roar in a most threatening manner but who was blissfully content the moment one gave him one's finger to suck. "Whiskey" got a good view of Paris during the few days he was there, for someone in the crowd was always borrowing him to take him some place. He, like most lions in captivity, became acquainted with bars, but the sort "Whiskey" saw were not for purposes of confinement.

The orders came directing the *escadrille* to Luxeuil and bidding farewell to gay "Paree" the men boarded the Belfort train with bag and baggage—and the lion. Lions, it developed, were not allowed in passenger coaches. The conductor was assured that "Whiskey" was quite harmless and was going to overlook the rules when the cub began to roar and tried to get at the railwayman's finger. That settled it, so two of the men had to stay behind in order to crate up "Whiskey" and take him along the next day.

The *escadrille* was joined in Paris by Robert Rockwell, of Cincinnati, who had finished his training as a pilot, and was waiting at the Reserve (Robert Rockwell had gone to France to work as a surgeon in one of the American war hospitals. He disliked remaining in the rear and eventually enlisted in aviation)....

11—Story of Thrilling Moments in the Air

Dennis Dowd, of Brooklyn, N.Y., is so far, the only American volunteer aviator killed while in training. Dowd, who had joined the Foreign Legion, shortly after the war broke out, was painfully wounded during the offensive in Champagne. After his recovery he was transferred, at his request, into aviation. At the Buc school, he stood at the head of the fifteen Americans who were learning to be aviators, and was considered one of the most promising pilots in the training camp. On August 11, 1916, while making a flight preliminary to his brevet, Dowd fell from a height of only 260 feet and was instantly killed. Either he had fainted or a control had broken.

While a patient at the hospital Dowd had been sent packages by a young French girl of Neuilly. A correspondence ensued, and when Dowd went to Paris on convalescent leave he and the young lady became engaged. He was killed just before the time set for the wedding....

In a few days, everyone in this Anglo-American alliance was calling each other by some nickname and swearing lifelong friendship.

"We didn't know what you Yanks would be like," remarked one of the Englishmen one day. "Thought you might be snobby on account of being volunteers, but I swear you're a bloody human lot." That, I will explain, is a very fine compliment....

Considering the number of machines that were continually roaring above the field at Luxeuil it is remarkable that only two fatal accidents occurred. One was when a British pilot tried diving at a target, for machinegun practice, and was unable to redress his airplane. Both he and his gunner were killed. In the second accident, I lost a good friend—a young Frenchman. He took up his gunner in a two-seated Nieuport. A young Canadian pilot accompanied by a French officer followed in a Sopwith. When at about a thousand feet they began to manoeuvre about one another. In making a turn too close the tips of their wings touched. The Nieuport turned downward, its wings folded, and it fell like a stone. The Sopwith fluttered a second or two, then its wings buckled and it dropped in the wake of the Nieuport. The two men in each of the planes were killed outright.

Next to falling in flames a drop in a wrecked machine is the worst death an aviator can meet. I know of no sound more horrible than that made by an airplane crashing to earth. Breathless one has watched the uncontrolled apparatus tumble through the air. The agony felt by the pilot and passenger seems to transmit itself to you. You are helpless to avert the certain death. You cannot even turn your eyes away at the moment of impact. In the dull, grinding crash there is the sound of breaking bones....

In spite of their bombardment of open towns and the use of explosive bullets in their aerial machine guns, the Boches have shown up in a better light in aviation than in any other arm. A few of the Hun pilots have evinced certain elements of honour and decency. I remember one chap that was the right sort.

He was a young man but a pilot of long standing. An old infantry captain stationed near his aviation field at Etain, east of Verdun, prevailed upon this German pilot to take him on a flight. There was a new machine to test out and he told the captain to climb aboard. Foolishly he crossed the trench lines and, actuated by a desire to give his passenger an interesting trip, proceeded to fly over the French aviation headquarters. Unfortunately for him he encountered three French fighting planes which promptly opened fire.

The German pilot was wounded in the leg and the gasoline tank of his airplane was pierced. Under him was an aviation field. He decided to land. The machine was captured before the Germans had time to burn it up. Explosive bullets were discovered in the machine gun. A French officer turned to the German captain and informed him that he would probably be shot for using explosive bullets. The captain did not understand.

"Don't shoot him," said the pilot, using excellent French, "if you're going to shoot anyone take me. The captain has nothing to do with the bullets. He doesn't even know how to work a machine gun. It's his first trip in an airplane."

"Well, if you'll give us some good information, we won't shoot you," said the French officer.

"Information," replied the German, "I can't give you any. I come from Etain, and you know where that is as well as I do."

"No, you must give us some worthwhile information, or I'm afraid you'll be shot," insisted the Frenchman.

"If I give you worthwhile information," answered the pilot, "you'll go over and kill a lot of soldiers, and if I don't you'll only kill one—so go ahead."

The last time I heard of the Boche he was being well taken care of.

12—Story of Rockwell's Last Fight

Kiffin Rockwell and Lufbery were the first to get their new machines ready and on the 23rd of September went out for the first flight since the *escadrille* had arrived at Luxeuil. They became separated in the air but each flew on alone, which was a dangerous thing to do in the Alsace sector. . . .

Just before Kiffin Rockwell reached the lines he spied a German machine under him flying at 11,000 feet. I can imagine the satisfaction he felt in at last catching an enemy plane in our lines. Rockwell had fought more combats than the rest of us put together, and had shot down many German machines that had fallen in their lines, but this was the first time he had had an opportunity of bringing down a Boche in our territory.

A captain, the commandant of an Alsatian village, watched the aerial battle through his field glasses. He said that Rockwell approached so close to the enemy that he thought there would be a collision. The German craft, which carried two machine guns, had opened a rapid fire when Rockwell started his dive. He plunged through the stream of lead and only when very close to his enemy did he begin shooting. For a second it looked as though the German was falling, so the captain said, but then he saw the French machine turn rapidly nose down, the wings of one side broke off and fluttered in the wake of the airplane, which hurtled earthward in a rapid drop.

It crashed into the ground in a small field—a field of flowers—a few hundred yards back of the trenches. It was not more than two and a half miles from the spot where Rockwell, in the month of May, brought down his first enemy machine. The Germans immediately opened up on the wreck with artillery fire.

In spite of the bursting shrapnel, gunners from a nearby battery rushed out and recovered poor Rockwell's broken body. There was a hideous wound in his breast where an explosive bullet had torn through. A surgeon who examined the body, testified that if it had been an ordinary bullet Rockwell would have had an even chance of landing with only a bad wound. As it was he was killed the instant the unlawful missile exploded.

Lufbery engaged a German craft but before he could get to close range two *Fokkers* swooped down from behind and filled his aeroplane full of holes. Exhausting his ammunition, he landed at Fontaine, an aviation field near the lines. There he learned of Rockwell's death and was told that two other French machines had been brought down within the hour. He ordered his gasoline tank filled, procured a full band of cartridges and soared up into the air to avenge his comrade. He sped up and down the lines, and made a wide detour to Habsheim where the Germans have an aviation field, but all to no avail. Not a Boche was in the air.

The news of Rockwell's death was telephoned to the *escadrille*. The captain, lieutenant, and a couple of men jumped in a staff car and hastened to where he had fallen. On their return, the American pilots were convened in a room of the hotel and the news broken to them. With tears in his eyes the captain said: "The best and bravest of us all is no more."

No greater blow could have befallen the *escadrille*. Kiffin was its soul. He was loved and looked up to by not only every man in our flying corps but by everyone who knew him. Kiffin was imbued with the spirit of the cause for which he fought and gave his heart and soul to the performance of his duty. He said: "I pay my part for Lafayette and Rochambeau," and he gave the fullest measure. The old flame of chivalry burned brightly in this boy's fine and sensitive being. With his death France lost one of her most valuable pilots.

When he was over the lines the Germans did not pass—and he was over them most of the time. He brought down four enemy planes that were credited to him officially, and Lieutenant de Laage, who was his fighting partner, says he is convinced that Rockwell accounted for many others which fell too far within the German lines to be observed. Rockwell had been given the *Médaille Militaire* and the *Croix de Guerre*, on the ribbon of which he wore four palms, representing the four magnificent citations he had received in the order of the army. As a further reward for his excellent work he had been proposed for promotion from the grade of sergeant to that of second lieutenant. Unfortunately, the official order did not arrive until a few days following his death.

The night before Rockwell was killed he had stated that if he were brought down he would like to be buried where he fell. It was impossible, however, to place him in a grave so near the trenches. His body was draped in a French flag and brought back to Luxeuil. He was given a funeral worthy of a general. His brother, Paul, who had fought in the Legion with him, and who had been rendered unfit for service by a wound, was granted permission to attend the obsequies.

Pilots from all nearby camps flew over to render homage to Rockwell's remains. Every Frenchman in the aviation at Luxeuil marched behind the bier. The British pilots, followed by a detachment of five hundred of their men, were in line, and a battalion of French troops brought up the rear. As the slow-moving procession of blue and khaki-clad men passed from the church to the graveyard, airplanes circled at a feeble height above and showered down myriads of flowers.

Rockwell's death urged the rest of the men to greater action, and the few who had machines were constantly after the Boches. Prince brought one down. Lufbery, the most skilful and successful fighter in the *escadrille*, would venture far into the enemy's lines and spiral down over a German aviation camp, daring the pilots to venture forth. One day he stirred them up, but as he was short of fuel he had to make for home before they took to the air. Prince was out in search of a combat at this time. He got it. He ran into the crowd Lufbery had aroused. Bullets cut into his machine and one exploding on the front edge of a lower wing broke it. Another shattered a supporting mast. It was a miracle that the machine did not give way. As badly battered as it was Prince succeeded in bringing it back from over Mulhouse, where the fight occurred, to his field at Luxeuil.

13—Story of Lufbery's Daring Flight

The same day that Prince was so nearly brought down Lufbery missed death by a very small margin. He had taken on more gasoline and made another sortie. When over the lines again he encountered a German with whom he had a fighting acquaintance. That is, he and the Boche, who was an excellent pilot, had tried to kill each other on one or two occasions before. Each was too good for the other. Lufbery manoeuvred for position but, before he could shoot, the Teuton would evade him by a clever turn. They kept after one another, the Boche retreating into his lines. When they were nearing Habsheim, Lufbery glanced back and saw French shrapnel bursting over the trenches. It meant a German plane was over French territory and it was his duty to drive it off. Swooping down near his adversary he waved goodbye, the enemy pilot did likewise, and Lufbery whirred off to chase the other representative of *Kultur*.

He caught up with him and dove to the attack, but he was surprised by a German he had not seen. Before he could escape three bullets entered his motor, two passed through the fur-lined combination he wore, another ripped open one of his woollen flying boots, his airplane was riddled from wing tip to wing tip, and other bullets cut the elevating plane. Had he not been an exceptional aviator he never would have brought safely to earth so badly damaged a machine. It was so thoroughly shot up that it was junked as being beyond repairs. Fortunately, Lufbery was over French territory or his forced descent would have resulted in his being made prisoner.

I know of only one other airplane that was safely landed after receiving as heavy punishment as did Lufbery's. It was a two-place Nieuport piloted by a young Frenchman named Fontaine with whom I trained. He and his gunner attacked a German over the Bois le Pretre who drove rapidly far into his lines. Fontaine followed and in turn was attacked by three other Boches. He dropped to escape, they plunged after him forcing him lower. He looked and saw a German aviation field under him. He was by this time only 2,000 feet above the ground. Fontaine saw the mechanics rush out to grasp him, thinking he would land. The attacking airplanes had stopped shooting. Fontaine pulled on full power and headed for the lines.

The German planes dropped down on him and again opened fire. They were on his level, behind and on his sides. Bullets whistled by him in streams. The rapid-fire gun on Fontaine's machine had jammed and he was helpless. His gunner fell forward on him, dead. The trenches were just ahead, but as he was slanting downward to gain speed he had lost a good deal of height, and was at only six hundred feet when he crossed the lines, from which he received a ground fire. The Germans gave up the chase and Fontaine landed with his dead gunner. His wings were so full of holes that they barely supported the machine in the air,

14—Story of a Surprise Attack on the Boches

The uncertain wait at Luxeuil finally came to an end on the 12th of October. The afternoon of that day the British did not say: "Come on Yanks, let's call off the war and have tea," as was their wont, for the bombardment of Oberndorf was on. The British and French machines had been prepared. Just before climbing into their airplanes the pilots were given their orders. The English in their single-seated Sopwiths, which carried four bombs each, where the first to leave. The big French *Breguets* and *Farmans* then soared aloft with their tons of explosive destined for the Mauser works. The fighting machines, which were to convoy them as far as the Rhine, rapidly gained their height and circled above their charges. Four of the battle planes were from the American *escadrille*. They were piloted respectively by Lieutenant de Laage, Lufbery, Norman Prince, and Masson.

The Germans were taken by surprise and as a result few of their machines were in the air. The bombardment fleet was attacked, however, and six of its planes shot down, some of them falling in flames. Baron, the famous French night bombarder, lost his life in one of the *Farmans*. Two Germans were brought down by machines they attacked and the four pilots from the American *escadrille* accounted for one each. Lieutenant de Laage shot down his Boche as it was attacking another French machine and Masson did likewise. Explaining it afterward he said: "All of a sudden I saw a Boche come in between me and a *Breguet*, I was following. I just began to shoot, and darned if he didn't fall."

As the fuel capacity of a Nieuport allows but little more than two hours in the air the *avions de chasse* were forced to return to their own lines to take on more gasoline, while the bombardment planes continued on into Germany. The Sopwiths arrived first at Oberndorf. Dropping low over the Mauser works they discharged their bombs and headed homeward. All arrived, save one, whose pilot lost his way and came to earth in Switzerland. When the big machines got to Oberndorf they saw only flames and smoke where once the rifle factory stood. They unloaded their explosives on the burning mass.

The Nieuports having refilled their tanks went up to clear the air of Germans that might be hovering in wait for the returning raiders. Prince found one and promptly shot it down. Lufbery came upon three. He drove for one, making it drop below the others, then forcing a second to descend, attacked the one remaining above. The combat was short and at the end of it the German tumbled to earth. This made the fifth enemy machine which was officially credited to Lufbery. When a pilot has accounted for five Boches he is mentioned by name in the official communication, and is spoken of as an "Ace," which in French aerial slang means a super-pilot.

Papers are allowed to call an "ace" by name, print his picture and give him a write-up. The successful aviator becomes a national hero. When Lufbery worked into this category the French papers made him a head liner. The American "Ace," with his string of medals, then came in for the *ennuis* of a matinee idol. The choicest bit in the collection was a letter from Wallingford, Conn., his home town, thanking him for putting it on the map.

15—Story of the Last Fight of Norman Prince

Darkness was coming rapidly on but Prince and Lufbery remained in the air to protect the bombardment fleet. Just at nightfall Lufbery made for a small aviation field near the lines, known as Corcieux. Slow-moving machines, with great planing capacity, can be landed in the dark, but to try and feel for the ground in a Nieuport, which comes down at about a hundred miles an hour, is to court disaster. Ten minutes after Lufbery landed Prince decided to make for the field. He spiralled down through the night air and skimmed rapidly over the trees bordering the Corcieux field.

In the dark, he did not see a high-tension electric cable that was stretched just above the tree tops. The landing gear of his airplane struck it. The machine snapped forward and hit the ground on its nose. It turned over and over. The belt holding Prince broke and he was thrown far from the wrecked plane. Both of his legs were broken and he naturally suffered internal injuries.

In spite of the terrific shock and his intense pain Prince did not lose consciousness. He even kept his presence of mind and gave orders to the men who had run to pick him up. Hearing the hum of a motor, and realising a machine was in the air, Prince told them to light gasoline fires on the field. "You don't want another fellow to come down and break himself up the way I've done," he said.

Lufbery went with Prince to the hospital in Gerardmer. As the ambulance rolled along Prince sang to keep up his spirits. He spoke of getting well soon and returning to service. It was like Norman. He was always energetic about his flying. Even when he passed through the harrowing experience of having a wing shattered, the first thing he did on landing was to busy himself about getting another fitted in place and the next morning he was in the air again.

No one thought that Prince was mortally injured but the next day he went into a coma. A blood clot had formed on his brain. Captain Haff in command of the aviation groups of Luxeuil, accompanied by our officers, hastened to Gerardmer. Prince lying unconscious on his bed, was named a second lieutenant and decorated with the Legion of Honour. He already held the *Médaille Militaire* and *Croix de Guerre*. Norman Prince died on the 15th of October.

He was brought back to Luxeuil and given a funeral similar to Rockwell's. It was hard to realise that poor old Norman had gone. He was the founder of the American *escadrille* and every one in it had come to rely on him. He never let his own spirits drop, and was always on hand with encouragement for the others. I do not think Prince minded going. He wanted to do his part before being killed, and he had more than done it. He had, day after day, freed the line of Germans, making it impossible for them to do their work, and three of them he had shot to earth.

Two days after Prince's death the *escadrille* received orders to leave for the Somme. The night before the departure the British gave the American pilots a farewell banquet and toasted them as their "Guardian Angels." They keenly appreciated the fact that four men from the American escadrille had brought down four Germans, and had cleared the way for their squadron returning from Oberndorf. When the train pulled out the next day the station platform was packed by khaki-clad pilots waving goodbye to their friends the "Yanks."

The *escadrille* passed through Paris on its way to the Somme front. The few members who had machines flew from Luxeuil to their new post. At Paris, the pilots were re-enforced by three other American boys who had completed their training. They were: Fred Prince, who ten months before had come over from Boston to serve in aviation with his brother Norman; Willis Haviland, of Chicago, who left the American Ambulance for the life of a birdman, and Bob Soubrian, of New York, who had been transferred from the Foreign Legion to the flying corps after being wounded in the Champagne offensive. . . .

Knights of the Air—Frenchmen Who Defy Death

TALES OF VALOUR IN BATTLES OF THE CLOUDS
Told by the Fliers Themselves—and Eyewitnesses

These are, indeed, days of the new knighthood. No knights of old ever rode into the tournament with truer chivalry than the modern knights of the air. Thousands of tales could be told of them—for each flight is another Great Adventure. The gallant Italians in their flights over the Alps have surpassed the bravery of the old Romans. Among them are such men as D'Annunzio, the Italian poet. The Americans, British, Russians—throughout the armies of the Allies, these knights of the airships have met the knights of Germany and Austria in death-struggles in the clouds. It is not possible here to call the "roll of honour" of Guynemer, Nungesser, Navarre, Chaput, Chainat, Dorme, Lenoir, Rochefort Heurteaux—and a host of others. Only a few stories can be told of the chivalry of the Frenchmen to symbolise the staunch hearts of all the men who battle in the clods.

1—STORY OF GUYNEMER—LAST FLIGHT OF FRENCH DAREDEVIL

The dashing Guynemer, King of the Airmen, has made his last sensational "down," a victim of a German plane. "Ace of the Aces" has been missing since the latter part of September, 1917. When last observed he was engaged, single-handed, with a squadron of enemy planes numbering more than forty, and the last official communication in regard to him read: "Although all means of investigation have been tried, we have not obtained any further information." And so, it is feared that Capt. Georges Guynemer, the eagle of the birdmen, the Frenchman with the face of a woman and heart of a lion, has fought his last battle in the clouds.

Guynemer was one of the youngest men of his rank in the French Army, having been appointed by President Poincare in February at the age of twenty-two. It was his custom to operate alone, handling the wheel of his machine as well as his gun, and his wonderful aerial conquests made him a hero throughout France. All his short life he had been an invalid with a tendency to tuberculosis, and, believing that he would not live long, he determined to give his life to his country in a manner that would enable him to first accomplish the utmost to her advantage. A comrade thus described his last flight....

> Guynemer sighted five machines of the Albatross type *D-3*. Without hesitating, he bore down on them. At that moment enemy patrolling machines, soaring at a great height, appeared suddenly and fell upon Guynemer,
> There were forty enemy machines in the air at this time, including Count von Richthofen and his circus division of machines, painted in diagonal blue and white stripes. Toward Guynemer's right some Belgian machines hove in sight, but it was too late. Guynemer must have been hit. His machine dropped gently toward the earth, and I lost track of it. All that I can say is that the machine was not on fire.

Guynemer was last cited in the French official announcement of September 10, 1917, for having won his fiftieth aerial victory. In an unofficial dispatch, a few days before he was said to have accounted for fifty-two enemy planes. His German rival for the war-honours of the air, Baron von Richthofen, is credited with seventy "downs." But the German method of scoring such engagements differs materially from that of the French, inasmuch as a French aviator, in order to get credit for a victory, must send his victim's plane to destruction in sight of two official observers, while a German scores if he but send a bullet through his adversary's motor, forcing him to glide to the earth.

Guynemer had a fine courage as well as bravery, and a determined spirit that obtained for him entrance into the army after he had been several times rejected for lack of sufficient physique....

Captain Guynemer was only twenty-three years old. He was born on Christmas day, 1893, the son of a prosperous manufacturer of Compiegne, who had been a captain in the French Army. All his brief life he had been an invalid, very tall and very slender, even showing a leaning toward tuberculosis.

Under tutors Georges had studied to enter the Ecole Polytechnique of Paris, but was rejected because of his frail health. The professors did not believe he could live to finish the course, so why waste the time with him? His parents had taken the youth to Biarritz for his health, and they had been there a year when the Great War started. Five times the young man tried to enlist as a private in the French Army and each time he was rejected because of his health.

Certain there was something he could do for his country, young Guynemer volunteered for work in the aeroplane factories. His natural bent was mechanics and his progress was rapid. His superiors recognised the thorough elementary education he had. He had studied in England for two years and made a tour of the world in search of health, but always studying. He remained for a time in the United States.

Soon Georges Guynemer became a mechanician at the military aviation-fields, and there his work and his personal character so impressed the officers that he was permitted to enlist as a student aviator. That was his chance, and he made more of it than any other aviator ever did. He obtained a pilot's license in January, 1916, and as a sergeant made his first flight in an *avion de chasse*.

In less than three weeks he had brought down his fifth enemy aeroplane, thus becoming an Ace and earning an official citation. From the first his career was, perhaps, more active than that of any other aviator along the battle-front. His most spectacular feat, for which he was made a lieutenant and decorated with the Cross of War, was on September 29 last year, when he rose in the air to defend a comrade of his escadrille who had been attacked by five German *Fokkers*.

At a height of more than 10,000 feet Captain Guynemer shot and dropped two of the Germans within thirty seconds of each other. He then pursued the three others, and in two minutes had shot down his third enemy machine. He was pursuing the remaining two Fokkers when an enemy shell exploded under his aeroplane and tore away one wing.

"I felt myself dropping," he said later. "It was 10,000 feet to the earth. I pulled and pushed every lever I had, but nothing would check my terrific descent. Five thousand feet from the earth the wrecked machine began to turn somersaults, but I was strapped into the seat. I do not know what it was, but something happened and I felt the speed descent lessen. But suddenly there was a tremendous crash, and when I recovered my senses I had been taken from the wreckage and was all right."

Three times Captain Guynemer was wounded in battle, but each time slightly.

Many stories are told which illustrate the importance which the Germans attached to his flights and their efforts to "down" the fearless aviator, H. Massac Buist tells this story:

> A distinct feature of the French aviation service in 1917 is its treatment of 'star turns.' One of the most brilliant is a man who has been shot several times, whose nerves are seemingly of steel, and whose skill rather increases than diminishes with the number of occasions on which he issues from hospital.
> He is attached to no particular squadron. Instead, he is free to go of his own sweet will to any part of the front, from the Belgian coast to the Swiss frontier. The Germans attach so much importance to him that they follow his progress from point to point.
> One day the champion pilot elected to come where the British were. Within twenty-four hours of his arrival the enemy were on the alert for him. The Germans sent up ten machines to catch him. Single-handed he set out for them, and promptly brought down three.
> He travels in his personal automobile with his *chef*. The aeroplane he uses is always specially built to his own ideas. It is fitted with all manner of peculiar contrivances. When not engaging the enemy, in flying hours, it is his habit to take every opportunity to practise behind the scenes.

The story of the young airman's persistent and finally successful efforts to enter the aviation service is here told ...

> One of the members of the *N-3* spoke to me of the early days when Guynemer was so nearly driven away from the gates of the aerodrome.
> You should have seen him, eh? A stripling of nineteen who knew how to fly and insisted. He was just from the *lycée*; he had been rejected four times, but he insisted and he came to Pau to the aerodrome. *Eh bien*, they let him in at last, and I will tell you what he did. I went up with him once, after we were both aces, to get some photographs, because I understand photography. And the last thing he said to me was: 'Old fellow, I give you warning. Today I dodge no shells. Today is my anniversary.'
> Well, we went up and they recognised him—they always do,

because he flies like no one else in the world. Never have I heard such a cracking of shells. They started in a big circle all around us and came nearer and nearer, but he did not move. On the course he kept, and I—took photographs. At last I report that I have enough; but, no, he asks me to take some photographs of the puffy clouds around our plane. And when that is done he starts home again, but turns again and does a spiral, I do not know how many times, right over one of the batteries which had been looking for us. In the line, they thought he was crazy. But I knew well enough that Guynemer was paying us out for his early days when we dared to patronise him!

Guynemer's development was coincident with that of the light aircraft of the Nieuport type. In the little machine with the clipped wings that must take the earth at sixty miles an hour because it has no buoyancy at a lesser speed, Guynemer was at home. He won his "aceship" in a slower type, but his developed tactics required a craft that could make its 10,000 feet in ten minutes, and maintain a speed of 120 miles an hour.

Estimates based on the carrying capacity of the machines that Guynemer destroyed credit the captain with accounting for more than eighty pilots, observers, and gunners, all told. It was Guynemer who shot down Lieutenant Hohendorf, pilot for a French aeroplane factory before the war, who had destroyed twelve French machines. It is not impossible that Guynemer himself was an unfortunate victim added to the record of Richthofen's squad.

(For further details see *Guynemer: Chevalier of the Air* by Henry Bordeaux & Mary R. Parkman and *Richthofen & Böelcke in Their Own Words* by Manfred Freiherr von Richthofen & Oswald Böelcke published by Leonaur).

2—Story of Dorcieres—Duellist of the Clouds

For a generation Rouzier Dorcieres has been one of the most picturesque figures in Parisian life, holding the unique position of the dean of duellists. A dinner was given to him in April, 1911, by two hundred and fifty men, every one of whom had either fought a duel with him, been his or his opponent's second in a duel, been seconded by him, or had participated as principal or second in a duel he "directed." All told, he had been director of 267 sword or pistol combats, and of the occasions on which he had played the role of second he had completely lost count. He himself had fought no fewer than twenty-five duels, fifteen with the sword and ten with the pistol.

It is not surprising, then, that such a firebrand volunteered to serve France in arms when the war broke out, though he had passed the age limit set by the order of mobilization. Bulletins announced that fact at the time, and added that he had been attached to the aviation service. Bulletins equally brief announced that Dorcieres was "missing"—presumably either dead or wounded. No further details have been given of his fate until this story of the dramatic end of a remarkable man.

★★★★★★

On the night of August 2, 1914, Dorcieres and a few of his old cronies—old because all of the younger men who had consorted with him were mustered into the army—gathered at their table in their favourite *café*.

"My friends," said Dorcieres, as calmly as though he had been announcing that he was going to Deauville for a holiday at the seaside, "I bid you farewell. Tonight, I am going to volunteer as a soldier of France.

"You may wonder why, at the age of thirty-nine, I voluntarily enlist in the army, and why I choose to enter the aviation service, distinctly the place for a youth. Listen, then. You have always believed that I have never suffered an affront in my life that was not avenged. But there was one time when I was insulted—grossly—and the man who did it escaped me. Do you remember the winter, five years ago, that I passed in Switzerland? It was there, when I was stopping in Zurich, that the thing occurred. It was after dinner, when the man sitting next to me nudged my shoulder.

"'So, you are Rouzier Dorcieres,' he said. 'I recognise you. And they say you have never been touched in a duel. Well, I am sorry I have never had the good fortune to meet you in one.' Then he laughed a sneering laugh.

"My blood boiled. 'But you will have the chance to meet me tomorrow morning,' I replied, glaring at him for his insolence. And then as I surveyed his countenance I saw the answer for his piggishness. He was a Prussian.

"'No,' he answered me, 'I will not be able to avail myself of the pleasure of measuring swords with you, as I leave for Germany on the midnight train. I am attached to the Imperial Aviation Corps and must report at Johannisthal tomorrow.'

"I looked at my watch. It was but a few minutes after eight o'clock. 'Then I will teach you your lesson tonight,' I told him.

"'*Monsieur*,' he said, 'I shall meet you here before ten o'clock with my seconds and the swords. We will settle this affair before I depart.'

"I bowed with pleasure as he stalked from the restaurant. And then whom did I see sitting near me but our old friend, the Comte de B——, as fine a second as any man ever had. In a few words, I had recounted the incident and called on him to act in my behalf. I waited in that restaurant with the *comte* until eleven o'clock. The Prussian officer did not appear. Two years afterward I read in a dispatch from Berlin of his being brevetted as an aviator in the *Kaiser's* service, and recently I read of how he was working in the air-service of the German Army.

"That is why I enter the aviation service of France. Because I still hope to meet him and make him repay his debt of honour to me."

Dorcieres went to the front to seek in the air the only man who had ever insulted him and failed to pay the price. His pilot, the aviator who operated the aeroplane in which he fought his last duel, told the rest of the story to Dorcieres's friends long after the official bulletins had announced his death:

"He told me to find you, *messieurs*, and to tell you just what he told me as he lay dying—dying from eleven machine-gun bullets which riddled his torso in that last combat which nearly cost me, also, my life.

"Rouzier Dorcieres was the strangest machine-gunner I ever had with me. Unlike other gunners, he always carried binoculars, and when we sighted and approached a Boche aeroplane he spent his preliminary time in peering intently at the occupants of the enemy machine instead of preparing and testing his *mitrailleuse* anxiously as most gunners do.

"As we circled near the German machine in his last flight Dorcieres passed me a scrap of paper. On it he had scrawled a request that I swoop past the German as near as I could. Instantly I divined his reason—and his reason for always carrying and using his high-power glasses. He thought he recognised one of the occupants of the other aeroplane.

"I swerved and doubled and shot past the *Fokker's* tail. Dorcieres's eyes bad been riveted to the glasses, but he dropped them now, heedlessly, and they smashed in the bottom of the fuselage.

"Dorcieres's right hand was on the *mitrailleuse*-trigger and his left was feeding the cartridge-belt cleanly into the loading-chamber as we rounded and flashed by, abreast, but a little higher, than the enemy.

"*Taca-tac-pouf-pouf-taca-tac-pouf-pouf*—and he drove thirty rounds at the *Fokker*. And then as I swerved the Boche turned upward and let fly at us. He had been traveling faster than I thought, because my mind had been distracted by approaching too near him at Dorcieres's request, and he reached us with every shot from his machine gun. Our fuselage cracked and splintered as the leaden hail perforated the car and the choking gasps that I heard behind me were the positive indications that my gunner had been hit. I, too, turned upward, as my motor was undamaged and climbed with the German. Then we both planed and approached each other. I heard my *mitrailleuse* begin to spit at the exact fraction of a second that we came within range, and the enemy gun never once barked a reply. Dorcieres's first shot must have killed the enemy gunner. And his torrent of bullets ripped off the tail of the *Fokker* and it dived into our lines like a stone, nose down.

"I landed within fifty yards of the broken Boche car and its occupants. Two stretchers were waiting there for us, but I was unhurt, miraculously. We put Dorcieres in one, tenderly as a baby, and then started off. But he had seen the wreck of the *Fokker* there and he begged that we stop beside it.

"Beside the German machine were the pilot and the gunner, both dead. By a superhuman effort my dying gunner raised himself on his elbow. He gazed at the face of the enemy machine-gunner.

"'It is he,' was all he said. And we carried him to the field-hospital.

"That afternoon I went to see him. He was pretty nearly gone. That is when he explained, and that is when he asked me to convey to you, *messieurs*, this message—that he had avenged his honour."

These stories of the aviators could be told indefinitely; how they met in mortal combats in the clouds; how they act as sky-pilots for the armies; how they raided the Krupp gun works; how they soar over the navies, but they must be left for future volumes for they are creating a history of their own—one of the most remarkable in the annals of war.

Tales of German Air Raiders over London and Paris

"How We Drop Bombs on the Enemies' Cities"
Told by the Air Raiders Themselves

The first stirring sensations of the Great War, which aroused the imaginations of the people, were the sailing of the fleets of ships in the air and under the seas. The world was indeed startled when the squadrons of Zeppelins rose from Germany, crossed the seas, and hovered over England, dropping bombs on ports and cities, and hurling death from the clouds. Here are two stories of German raiders in which they tell how it feels to drop bombs from the skies on European capitals. The German authorities permitted the publication in a Hamburg newspaper of a very exciting and detailed account of a Zeppelin raid upon London by one of the crew of the airship. This account was designed to arouse the enthusiasm of the German nation for the daring and difficult work done by the Zeppelins, and to make them realize the havoc and terror they created in England. A translation of the narrative follows:

1—How We Zeppelined the Heart of London
Told by Commander of a German Air Fleet

Our Zeppelin received orders at 6 o'clock in the evening to fly from our hangar in Belgium for an attack on London.

The giant airship slipped easily out of the long shed with noiseless motors, and after rising to 8,000 feet, the altitude most suited for steady flying, our captain steered by compass straight for London.

Our true German hearts beat high this night with the hope of doing some great and irreparable damage to London. . . .

Perhaps we should destroy their House of Parliament.... or their War Office.... or the Foreign Office ... or the official dwellings of the Prime Minister and the Chancellor of the Exchequer.... Well did I know the location of all these places from my long residence in London.

Our commander said that a bomb dropped in a certain space of half a square mile in London could hardly fail to destroy some person of great importance in the official or wealthy classes of England.

Perhaps we might strike a school or a hospital or a party of women. We should regret such accidents, but it is impossible to modify our splendid and effective aerial warfare simply because innocent combatants place themselves in the way of legitimate objects of attack.... We know that London is a fortified city, and non-combatants who remain there do so at their own peril.

The way had for months been prepared by previous aerial attacks and reconnoissances for a more accurate and effective blow at the heart of London. All lights, both street lamps and those in dwellings, have been lowered by order of the English Government to a point that causes the busiest thoroughfare at night to present only a dull glow a few hundred yards away.

On the other hand, powerful searchlights operated in connection with anti-aircraft guns, and other military works are kept constantly playing on the sky in the search for our airships. If we can discover the topographical position of these searchlights and batteries we can establish the other principal centres of the city from them and throw our bombs with some approach to accuracy—that is to say, we can at least drop them on a quarter where we know that there are public buildings or where important officials reside.

To establish the location of these points has been the work of our earlier air reconnoissances, and as a result of this system our work must become more and more deadly every day. We have, for instance, found that powerful searchlights and batteries are operated at Woolwich on the extreme eastern outskirts of London, at St. James's Park, which is in the centre of the metropolis, at Hampstead Heath on the north, and at the Crystal Palace, south of the Thames. The English are not likely to move all these defensive points, and if one is moved and not the others, the captain of the Zeppelin can discover the change by reference to the other points.

As our Zeppelin can travel seventy miles an hour at its maximum, the journey of a little more than two hundred miles from Belgium could be performed in a few hours. Darkness was falling as we passed over the stormy North Sea for we did not wish to be seen and reported by patrol ships.

The cold was intense and could be felt through the fleece-lined clothes and heavy felt shoes with which we were provided. Our Zeppelin carried four tons of the most destructive explosives ever created by science—sufficient to annihilate the heart of London, the greatest city in the world. The amount was divided into forty bombs of 100 pounds each, and eighty of fifty pounds each. The larger bombs are designed to destroy fortifications and heavy buildings. The smaller ones are for the purpose of setting fire to houses, and contain an explosive that develops a temperature of 5,000 degrees Fahrenheit.

We made out the mouth of the Thames from certain lightships and shore lights that have been maintained. At about 10 o'clock we found a powerful searchlight playing on us. This we knew from our information to be Woolwich, the important English arsenal. As we no longer desired to conceal our presence, we discharged ten of the larger bombs in the vicinity of the searchlight.

The bombs are discharged from tubes pointing downward from a steel plate in the floor of the airship. The bomb is furnished with a steel handle, and by means of this it is lowered into the tube. A bolt fitting into a hole in the bomb holds it in the tube. The marksman presses his foot on an electric button in the plate in the floor of the car and this withdraws the bolt, releasing the bombs. He can drop two bombs at once if he wishes, and the third two seconds later.

The height at which the airship flies, its speed and the effects of wind at present render impossible scientific aim in the sense that an artillerist would use the term. Nevertheless, a considerable degree of effectiveness is attained by Zeppelin marksmen, while a poor marksman may entirely waste his ammunition. To hit a mark half an acre in extent is good marksmanship from a Zeppelin. In practice, a regiment of wooden dummies was set up in a field and one of our aerial marksmen succeeded in wiping out the whole regiment.

If Zeppelin marksmanship is still rudimentary, the destructive power of our bombs, on the other hand, is terrible beyond anything dreamed of before this war. One of our 100-pound bombs striking fairly will destroy any existing building not constructed purely as a fortification. Even if it strikes in a street, it will dig a hole a hundred feet deep, destroying gas pipes, electric wire conduits, subways and any subterranean constructions that may be beneath the surface. Thus, the destruction and paralyzing of all life in a city can be practically assured if we use sufficient bombs. Our bombardment of Woolwich was followed by the extinction of the searchlight, and we had reason to believe that we had inflicted serious damage at this important centre.

We knew that in a few minutes we should be over the heart of London. Our daring commander decided to sail very low, following the course of the Thames which he knew would take him near all the objects he wished to reach.

Suddenly the huge outline of a building loomed under our noses. Seen against the dull, cloudy sky, it appeared colossal. We almost struck it. It was a church! It was St. Paul's Cathedral! An instantaneous turn of the elevating rudder saved us from a collision with the monstrous dome. A few seconds more straight to the westward and we knew that we were over the centre of official and fashionable London.

Our commander ordered the bombs discharged as fast as we could throw them. The ship circled slowly round and round, peppering death on the solar plexus of the British Empire.

Beneath us was the Strand, with its theatres and hotels, the House of Parliament, the Government offices in Whitehall and Parliament street, the residences of the aristocracy in Mayfair, the fashionable clubs in Pall Mall, Buckingham Palace, the War Office, the Admiralty and Westminster Abbey.

It was a night of terror for London! The searchlights and the guns played upon us constantly. At night, the anti-aircraft fighters use shells that spread a long trail of luminous red smoke through the darkness in order to mark the position of the airship for the other gunners firing shrapnel. It was a grand and inconceivably weird spectacle to watch the electric beams and the long red trails playing about in the air, while shrapnel burst about us and our great bombs exploded on the earth below with a glow that we could faintly discern.

It is exceedingly difficult for a gunner to hit an airship at a height of 8,000 feet, or even lower. We enjoyed a feeling of tremendous power and security. Our daring commander ordered our craft to circle lower and lower in his determination to inflict the greatest possible injury on the enemy.

At last we could see the outlines of buildings on the ground. Below us was a great open square and in the centre a very high slender column. It was the ... British monument to their noted Admiral Nelson standing in the centre of Trafalgar Square.

"Give old Nelson a bomb!" roared our brave commander.

Down went a bomb aimed straight at the head of the one-eyed admiral. The fervent wishes of every man in our crew went with it. Whether it struck the mark time alone will show.

We had ventured too near the earth, and an unusually well-aimed shot struck the forward part of our vessel. One of our mechanical experts, in his anxiety to ascertain the nature of the damage, climbed out on a stay, fell and was, of course, lost. That was our only casualty. We found later that the shot had only penetrated one "*ballonnet*" and had not interfered with our stability in any important degree.

Our commander threw the elevating rudders to their extreme upward angle, and in a few minutes, we were practically out of danger once more. We threw all our supply of bombs upon London and then turned for home again. Steering by compass and the stars for Belgium, we made the return journey without mishap. The dawn was just breaking when we came in sight of certain landmarks which guided us to our hangar.

There are certain details of the raid which I should not wish to reveal, and could not reveal without making myself liable to the death penalty. An attack by a Zeppelin is always accompanied by other air craft, both dirigibles and aeroplanes, in order to give protection to our capital airships and create confusion among the enemy. The English never know whether they are firing at a Zeppelin or a semi-rigid dirigible of similar shape, but comparatively small importance. These are the scouting cruisers of the air. Moreover, our raiding forces split up in the darkness according to pre-arranged plans, thus causing hopeless confusion among our terrestrial opponents, even if the approaching attack has been reported to them in advance.

2—How It Feels to Drop Bombs on Paris

Told by a Young German Aeronaut in a Letter to His Mother

Dear Mother:

Thank God! After a veritable Odyssy, today at noon I again reached my division. With much joy, I was greeted on all sides, for, after a four days' absence I was given up for lost. Dear little mother, I shall tell you the story from the beginning. During the forenoon, I went up at D—— for the purpose of ascertaining the enemy's position at L—— and F——, and to take notes on their movements. Ober-Lieutenant K—— went along as observer, and my biplane soon carried us to a height of about 800 metres above the enemy's position, which was sketched and photographed time and again.

As expected, we were soon the object of a lively firing, and several times I felt a well-known trembling in the machine—a sign that a shot had hit one of the wings. After a three-hour flight, we were able to give our reports to General Herringen at headquarters. He praised us warmly and ordered that we be served a roast chicken and he gave us some fine Havana cigars.

As I was again preparing my aeroplane in the afternoon, with the help of several chauffeurs, who filled the benzine tank, and as I was patching the four bullet holes with linen, a Bavarian officer told me that he would like to observe the retreat of the English from the large pike toward M——. I prepared my machine immediately, and around 4 o'clock, with Major G——, I went up. By following the streets, it was soon evident that the English retreat was without plan or order, but to all appearances the troops wanted to reach fortified positions as fast as they could. Perhaps they would flee all the way to Paris.

Paris! The Bavarian officer shrieking something to me. Though the motor almost drowned, I understood what he meant. I glanced at the benzine indicator. I possessed sufficient oil. Paris, it would be!

Steering toward the south, we journeyed for half an hour, and then out of the distance, far, far below, the grey stone housetops of the French capital took shape. Something impelled me to increase our speed, and we raced toward the city at seventy miles an hour. Incredibly fast Paris becomes clearer and more distinct.

The chain of the forts St. Denis! Montmartre stands out through the mist! The iron pillars of the Eifel Tower! . . . We are directly above Paris. The major points below with his finger; then he slowly turns to me, raises himself from his seat and shouts, "Hurrah!"

And I? From sheer joy, mother, I nearly went out of my mind. I began to make the wildest circles in the air. I felt I could do anything. There the white Sacred Heart Church, here the Gare du Nord, there Notre Dame, there the old *"Boul Mich,"* where as a student I had so often caroused and which now, as conqueror, I soared above.

The heart of the enemy seemed defenceless; the proud, gleaming Seine lay below me. Everything horrible which I always thought of Paris as possessing vanished—only an impression of the wonderful and the great remained; and I loved Paris more as a conqueror.

Over the housetops I swung in great circles. Little dots in the streets showed me that crowds were gathering. They could not understand how a German could handle the French invention more skilfully and advantageously than the French themselves. They began to shoot at us. It was fine. They were very bad shots. I felt like dropping a bomb—not to kill them, but simply to see something blown up. Then from the direction of Juvisy came a French monoplane. As it was more swift than my biplane, I had to turn and try to escape.

My Bavarian comrade prepared my rifle and seized his pistol. The Frenchman approached closer and closer. I attempted to reach the protecting clouds at 6,000 feet, but my pursuer flew swifter than we, ever nearer and nearer. Suddenly I became aware of a second monoplane only 500 yards away. It attempted to block my path. We had to act. I shot at the airman ahead of us. Then a turn and the major took aim. He shot once, twice, three times. The enemy's machine, which was now next to us only 100 yards away, toppled, tilted upward, and then fell to the ground like a stone. But our other pursuer was almost on top of us and shot at us with pistols. Close to the gas lever a bullet hit the fuselage. Then impenetrable fog concealed us from the enemy. I could hear the buzz of his motor grow fainter and fainter.

When we again emerged from this grey ocean of clouds it was twilight. But suddenly, before, behind and on the sides, white smoke clouds appeared bursting shrapnel. Still flying above the enemy's position, we were directly exposed to their artillery fire. Devil with it! The fire grew worse. I knew from the little trembles that the machine was getting blew upon blow, but it never entered my mind that those shrapnel balls meant death to me. Something in man remains unmoved by logic and knowledge—especially when you're in the air. There, of a sudden, a white-yellow fire in front of me. The machine reared up. The major seemed to reel to his feet. Blood was pouring from his shoulder. The covering of the wings was tattered. The motor buzzed and roared as before, but the screw was missing.

A *grenat* shattered our propeller, but, thank heaven, did no worse. My machine began sinking to earth. I succeeded in gliding and threw the biplane down into the woods. The branches and tree tops crashed to splinters. I struck the steering gear and then was no longer aware of what went on around me. When I again became conscious I was lying next to Major G——. on the forest ground surrounded by a group of German reservists. Recognising the machine, they had forced themselves into the forest in small numbers to save us. Major G—— had to be removed to the nearest hospital. I only received a crushed leg.

Your Affectionate Son.

The Aerial Attack on Ravenna
Told by Paolo Poletti

In *L'lllustrazione Italiana* this distinguished Italian author expresses his indignation at the bombardment of Ravenna by Austrian aviators, when the ancient Basilica of Sant' Apollinare narrowly escaped destruction. Translated for current history.

I write with a feeling of relief. My beautiful Sant' Apollinare is uninjured, or nearly so. A blind bomb may have furrowed the April sky of my city, in this marvellous foretaste of Spring; but the criminal attempt has been in vain. And, with me, innumerable citizens of Ravenna have breathed a sigh almost of content. It is true that there were human victims. But our pity for them is too deep for any comment to be adequate; the only way to commemorate them worthily is to avenge them. But it is not of this wrong we wish to speak today. We wish only to bring together and to distil into a brief comment the living essence of the spirit of Ravenna, as it has affirmed itself in this historic, solemn hour.

The people of Ravenna have felt a lightning flash of sudden revolt because of the outrage perpetrated on their monuments. The citizens of Ravenna, if they have not, for the antique glories of their city, the fully conscious veneration which we shall hardly expect to find among them, nevertheless do breathe in from these monuments a deep impression of exaltation and well-founded pride. Our readers will remember those *Monologues* which Gigi Easi wrote with such grace and such penetrating humour. In one, *The Art of Delivering a Monologue*, he introduces as speakers the inhabitants of the various capital cities of Italy, each of whom magnifies the beauty of his own city.

So, it happens that, along with the Florentine, the Neapolitan, the Venetian, and the rest, there is not lacking a good citizen of Ravenna who, with vibrant words and potent adjectives, in intense and enthusiastic exaltation, energetically affirms the supremacy of his mosaics and his basilicas. The scene is not only most exhilarating, but also, from the point of view of psychology, profoundly true. Our populace lives, and feels that it lives, with its mighty memories and with its great historic personages, whose moral significance at least it knows how to estimate, and whose remoter glory it understands by a kind of natural and traditional intuition, and respects it, I might almost say, by a distant residuum of atavistic suggestion.

Galla, daughter and sister of emperors; Theodoric sleeping, sleeping, according to these humble fancies, a secular sleep under his heavy monolith; Justinian, upraiser of precious churches and reviser of the imperial idea and the laws of Rome; Theodora, the dancing girl become a queen, speak a language incomprehensible to the rough minds of our people, yet a secret fascination emanates to them from the rich vaults, heavy with gold, of the antique basilicas; from those vaulted roofs toward which, in their time, rose the thunderous hosannas of triumphal victories, and the humble supplications of tragical misfortunes; those vaulted domes, dazzling with emerald and ruby, to which were raised hands wrung in despair and menace, or joined in the lowly adoration of prayer; toward which were raised foreheads tormented with gnawing hatred or consoled by illuminating love. . . .

The *basilica* of Theodoric, made the target of the iniquitous attempt of the Barbarians, ever speaks to the people in the mysterious tongue of days long gone. . . .

Oh, my beautiful Sant' Apollinare! we dreaded to see shattered thy gleaming mosaics; we dreaded to see cut in two and mutilated thy ten-centuries-oil campanile, which sends forth joyful peals in the luminous evenings of May; we feared that the voice would be stilled, which arises from thee, to chant a profound poem of history and of art.

We recall your founder, Theodoric, and his reign in Ravenna; his wise and successful attempt to bring together in peaceful relations the conquerors and the conquered, engrafting into the ultimate stem of Latin civilization the young shoot of fresh barbaric energy; so that his terrible invasion did not interrupt the continuity of history, but proceeded to develop harmoniously in the integration of the old Roman elements with the new, blended in a single composed form of enduring life.

Of the art which reminds us, through the verses of Gabriel d'Annunzio, of the millenary of Ravenna, one might also speak: of the

"Purple night, gleaming with gold"; of the Virgins of Sant' Apollinare, in Francesca's passionate speech:

"The Virgins of Sant' Apollinare burn not so bright in their heaven of gold"; and the prophecy:

> Oh, Prisca, another hero will draw the bow from thy desert toward the infinite. . . . Clad in armour, he awaits the new days; thy warrior awaits the certain dawn, when a voice through the desert paths shall call forth the ancestral valour!

We fit the augury to the new times; and, to meet the new Barbarians, we invoke the sacred vengeance of Italy here, from this furthest bourne of our Garibaldian land!

ALSO FROM LEONAUR
AVAILABLE IN SOFTCOVER OR HARDCOVER WITH DUST JACKET

THE FALL OF THE MOGHUL EMPIRE OF HINDUSTAN *by H. G. Keene*—By the beginning of the nineteenth century, as British and Indian armies under Lake and Wellesley dominated the scene, a little over half a century of conflict brought the Moghul Empire to its knees.

LADY SALE'S AFGHANISTAN *by Florentia Sale*—An Indomitable Victorian Lady's Account of the Retreat from Kabul During the First Afghan War.

THE CAMPAIGN OF MAGENTA AND SOLFERINO 1859 *by Harold Carmichael Wylly*—The Decisive Conflict for the Unification of Italy.

FRENCH'S CAVALRY CAMPAIGN *by J. G. Maydon*—A Special Correspondent's View of British Army Mounted Troops During the Boer War.

CAVALRY AT WATERLOO *by Sir Evelyn Wood*—British Mounted Troops During the Campaign of 1815.

THE SUBALTERN *by George Robert Gleig*—The Experiences of an Officer of the 85th Light Infantry During the Peninsular War.

NAPOLEON AT BAY, 1814 *by F. Loraine Petre*—The Campaigns to the Fall of the First Empire.

NAPOLEON AND THE CAMPAIGN OF 1806 *by Colonel Vachée*—The Napoleonic Method of Organisation and Command to the Battles of Jena & Auerstädt.

THE COMPLETE ADVENTURES IN THE CONNAUGHT RANGERS *by William Grattan*—The 88th Regiment during the Napoleonic Wars by a Serving Officer.

BUGLER AND OFFICER OF THE RIFLES *by William Green & Harry Smith*—With the 95th (Rifles) during the Peninsular & Waterloo Campaigns of the Napoleonic Wars.

NAPOLEONIC WAR STORIES *by Sir Arthur Quiller-Couch*—Tales of soldiers, spies, battles & sieges from the Peninsular & Waterloo campaingns.

CAPTAIN OF THE 95TH (RIFLES) *by Jonathan Leach*—An officer of Wellington's sharpshooters during the Peninsular, South of France and Waterloo campaigns of the Napoleonic wars.

RIFLEMAN COSTELLO *by Edward Costello*—The adventures of a soldier of the 95th (Rifles) in the Peninsular & Waterloo Campaigns of the Napoleonic wars.

AVAILABLE ONLINE AT **www.leonaur.com**
AND FROM ALL GOOD BOOK STORES